Atheism: A Very Short Introduction

VERY SHORT INTRODUCTIONS are for anyone wanting a stimulating and accessible way into a new subject. They are written by experts, and have been translated into more than 45 different languages.

The series began in 1995, and now covers a wide variety of topics in every discipline. The VSI library currently contains over 650 volumes—a Very Short Introduction to everything from Psychology and Philosophy of Science to American History and Relativity—and continues to grow in every subject area.

Very Short Introductions available now:

ABOLITIONISM Richard S. Newman
THE ABRAHAMIC RELIGIONS
   Charles L. Cohen
ACCOUNTING Christopher Nobes
ADOLESCENCE Peter K. Smith
ADVERTISING Winston Fletcher
AERIAL WARFARE Frank Ledwidge
AESTHETICS Bence Nanay
AFRICAN AMERICAN RELIGION
   Eddie S. Glaude Jr
AFRICAN HISTORY John Parker and
   Richard Rathbone
AFRICAN POLITICS Ian Taylor
AFRICAN RELIGIONS
   Jacob K. Olupona
AGEING Nancy A. Pachana
AGNOSTICISM Robin Le Poidevin
AGRICULTURE Paul Brassley and
   Richard Soffe
ALEXANDER THE GREAT
   Hugh Bowden
ALGEBRA Peter M. Higgins
AMERICAN BUSINESS HISTORY
   Walter A. Friedman
AMERICAN CULTURAL
   HISTORY Eric Avila
AMERICAN FOREIGN RELATIONS
   Andrew Preston
AMERICAN HISTORY
   Paul S. Boyer
AMERICAN IMMIGRATION
   David A. Gerber
AMERICAN LEGAL HISTORY
   G. Edward White

AMERICAN MILITARY HISTORY
   Joseph T. Glatthaar
AMERICAN NAVAL HISTORY
   Craig L. Symonds
AMERICAN POLITICAL HISTORY
   Donald Critchlow
AMERICAN POLITICAL PARTIES
   AND ELECTIONS L. Sandy Maisel
AMERICAN POLITICS
   Richard M. Valelly
THE AMERICAN PRESIDENCY
   Charles O. Jones
THE AMERICAN REVOLUTION
   Robert J. Allison
AMERICAN SLAVERY
   Heather Andrea Williams
THE AMERICAN SOUTH
   Charles Reagan Wilson
THE AMERICAN WEST
   Stephen Aron
AMERICAN WOMEN'S HISTORY
   Susan Ware
AMPHIBIANS T. S. Kemp
ANAESTHESIA Aidan O'Donnell
ANALYTIC PHILOSOPHY
   Michael Beaney
ANARCHISM Colin Ward
ANCIENT ASSYRIA Karen Radner
ANCIENT EGYPT Ian Shaw
ANCIENT EGYPTIAN ART AND
   ARCHITECTURE Christina Riggs
ANCIENT GREECE Paul Cartledge
THE ANCIENT NEAR EAST
   Amanda H. Podany

Available soon:

For more information visit our website

www.oup.com/vsi/

Julian Baggini

ATHEISM

A Very Short Introduction

SECOND EDITION

OXFORD
UNIVERSITY PRESS

OXFORD
UNIVERSITY PRESS

Great Clarendon Street, Oxford, OX2 6DP,
United Kingdom

Oxford University Press is a department of the University of Oxford.
It furthers the University's objective of excellence in research, scholarship,
and education by publishing worldwide. Oxford is a registered trade mark of
Oxford University Press in the UK and in certain other countries

First edition published 2003
This edition published 2021

Impression: 1

Published in the United States of America by Oxford University Press
198 Madison Avenue, New York, NY 10016, United States of America

British Library Cataloguing in Publication Data
Data available

Library of Congress Control Number: 2021931880

ISBN 978-0-19-885679-5

Printed in Great Britain by
Ashford Colour Press Ltd, Gosport, Hampshire

Links to third party websites are provided by Oxford in good faith and
for information only. Oxford disclaims any responsibility for the materials
contained in any third party website referenced in this work.

This book is dedicated to two people who helped make the VSI series so iconic.

The first is the late Philip Atkins, who made over 300 paintings especially for this series, including for this volume. I was delighted to meet him and even more pleased when he said I could have the original.

The second is George Miller, an excellent editor who conceived of the series and became a very good friend.

Contents

Preface

A walk on the dark side?

In the first decade of the 21st century at a family funeral in Italy, a cousin once asked if I was a Catholic. I had indeed been educated in a Roman Catholic primary school and had been baptized and confirmed. But no, I wasn't a Catholic now. Protestant then? she asked. No, not that either. There was a pause while she struggled to work out what possibilities were left. With a look of shock and horror she asked, '*Ateo?' Atheist?*

It is a sign of how much the world has changed over the last century that such expressions of disbelief at the very possibility of disbelief have become rare. Still, atheism retains something of a dangerous reputation. Back when I was at primary school, the very word would conjure up dark images of something sinister, evil, and threatening. To be good meant to believe in God and to obey his will, so any rejection of the Almighty was by definition a rejection of the good. Atheists could only belong to the dark side.

Even now, when I think of the word 'atheist', something of the dark smudge my Catholic mentors smeared over it remains. This stain is now but a residue, hardly noticeable to my conscious mind. But the negative link has been forged and my attention is often involuntarily drawn towards it, as the eye is to a barely

perceptible flaw that, once noticed, cannot be forgotten.
Mud sticks.

My experience could be unusual, but irrational prejudices forged
from early experiences are not. We human beings often claim that
it is our ability to think which distinguishes us from other animals.
We are *Homo sapiens* after all—*thinking* hominids. Yet even when
we are not in the firm grip of irrational or non-rational forces and
desires, our thinking is infused with and shaped by emotions,
often without us realizing it.

I draw attention to this because what follows is almost entirely
about the rational case for atheism. However, I am also aware that
we do not approach such issues with blank, open minds. We come
to them with prejudices, fears, and commitments. These can
interfere with clear thinking, leading us to prejudge issues and
reject arguments without good grounds. If you have a deep-rooted
image of atheists as miserable, pessimistic amoralists, then
rational arguments to the contrary may encounter deep
psychological resistance. Similarly, if you assume religious
believers are all stupid and gullible, you will be too inclined to
accept any argument that counts against them, however weak.

Sometimes when prejudices are exposed to reason they crumble.
Sometimes, however, it is precisely those beliefs that are not
founded on reason that have greatest immunity against the power
of rational argumentation. The grip such convictions have on us
can be strong and we cannot simply will them away. But we can
try to become aware of them and compensate for them. It is in
that spirit that I invite believers and non-believers alike to read
this book and consider atheism as if for the first time.

Acknowledgements

There are many people to thank for their contributions to making this book happen. For the first edition, they are above all Marilyn Mason for her initial suggestion that I might give it a go, Shelly Cox for commissioning it, and Katharine Reeve and Emma Simmons for seeing it through to publication. Marsha Filion deserves special mention for fighting the flab in the penultimate draft. Colleagues on the Humanist Philosophers Group also helped enrich my understanding of positive atheism. I would also like to thank David Nash and Roger Griffin for their advice on reading for the history chapter.

For this second edition I am indebted to Andrea Keegan, Jenny Nugée, Rebecca Parker, Latha Menon, Kim Behrens, and Saraswathi Rajan at OUP, as well as to an anonymous reviewer.

List of illustrations

Chapter 1
What is atheism?

Atheism defined

There is a sense in which atheism defines itself. The word derives from the Greek, combining the privative 'a', meaning 'not' or 'without', with the word 'theos' meaning God. Atheism is therefore simply the belief that there is no God or gods. (Henceforth I shall talk simply of belief in God, but most of the arguments of this book apply equally to monotheistic and polytheistic beliefs.)

On this understanding, atheism is a 'boringly negative view' as the philosopher Tim Crane puts it. 'It simply says something about what there is not.' Crane says that 'As an atheist, I am untroubled by the idea that atheism might be a negative doctrine.'

Crane is technically correct. Atheism, strictly speaking, is nothing more than disbelief in God. And if atheism did lack any positive beliefs, there would be nothing to say about what it stands *for*, only what it stands *against*. Such a purely negative atheism could be said to be parasitic on religion: if there were no theists, there wouldn't even be any atheists.

I think this view is profoundly mistaken. Its initial plausibility is based on a very crude piece of flawed reasoning we can call the etymological fallacy. This is the mistake of thinking that one can best understand what a word means by understanding its origin. But this is evidently not always true. If you go into an Italian restaurant and only know that 'tagliatelle' literally means 'little boot laces' you are not going to have much idea what you're going to eat if you order it. The mere fact that the word 'atheist' is constructed as a negation of theism is not enough to show that it is essentially negative.

Etymology aside, veganism illustrates how positive views can be given a wholly negative framing. In an omnivorous culture the term 'vegan' is understood largely negatively: not eating any animal products. But veganism can also be defined positively as a diet composed entirely of plants and it would be absurd to say that it is 'parasitic' on carnivorousness.

Like 'atheism', the term 'veganism' doesn't even tell you what vegans positively believe. As a matter of fact, however, the majority of vegans do tend to share one of a small number of specific beliefs and principles, refusing meat on animal rights, environmental, and/or health grounds. That is why in 2020 a British judge ruled that veganism, when held on moral grounds, was a philosophical belief and therefore protected by equality laws.

Similarly, although the concept of atheism tells you nothing about what atheists positively believe, they do tend to share a distinctive belief about the fundamental nature of the world. Indeed, this shared belief gives them more in common than vegans have, since their choices can be motivated by a number of different beliefs.

Casting atheism in a negative light is in fact no more than a historical accident. Consider this story, which begins as fact and ends as fiction.

In Scotland there is a deep lake called Loch Ness. Some believe that the loch contains a strange creature, known as the Loch Ness

Monster. Many claim to have seen it although no firm evidence of its existence has ever been presented. The majority of people in Scotland do not believe in this monster and think that the lake is like other lochs in the country. But that is not to say they have no beliefs about the lake other than the fact that it is devoid of mythical beasts. They believe that the lake is a natural phenomenon of a particular size, that certain fish live in it, and so on. It's just that these beliefs they have are so ordinary that they do not usually require elucidation.

Now imagine that the number of believers in the monster grows. Soon, a word is coined to describe them: they are mockingly called 'Nessies'. (Many names of religions started as mocking nicknames, including Methodist, Quaker, and Christian.) Despite the fact that there is no good evidence for the monster's existence, soon being a Nessie becomes the norm and the name ceases to be a joke. Now it is the people previously thought of as normal who are in the minority. They soon get their own name, 'Anessies', those who don't believe in the monster.

Is it true to say that the beliefs of Anessies are parasitic on those of the Nessies? That can't be true, because the Anessies' beliefs pre-date those of the Nessies. The key point is not one of chronology, however. The key is that the Anessies would have had exactly the same beliefs even if the Nessies had never existed. What the rise of the Nessies did was to give a name to a set of beliefs that had always existed but which was considered so unexceptional that it required no special label.

The moral of the story should be clear. Atheism is no more parasitic on religion than the beliefs of the Anessies are parasitic on those of the Nessies. The absurdity of saying otherwise is perhaps made most clear by considering what would happen if everyone ceased to believe in God. If atheism were parasitic on religion, then surely it could not exist without religion. But if religion died out, that clearly would not be the end of atheism but its triumph. If theists did not exist atheists still would, but perhaps there would be no special name for them. It is only because most people have tended to believe in gods and spirits that atheists are defined in terms of what they deny rather than what they believe. Atheists do not need religion and nor does atheism.

Positively naturalist

A clue to the nature of atheism's positive character can be found by thinking more about its negatives. The atheist's rejection of belief in God is usually accompanied by a broader rejection of any supernatural or transcendental reality. For example, an atheist does not usually believe in the existence of immortal souls, life after death, ghosts, or supernatural powers. Rather, the atheist is almost always a *naturalist*, believing that there is only the natural world and not any supernatural one. This is the belief the Anessies had before they were given their negative name. There are hardly any atheists who are not naturalists because the arguments and ideas that sustain atheism tend to support naturalism and rule out other beliefs in the supernatural or transcendental.

Naturalism is a broad family of positions which comes in stronger and weaker versions. Minimally, it is the claim that the natural world is all that there is. There are some who would consider themselves religious and naturalistic, seeing God and nature as one and the same. Spinoza's God, for example, is another word for nature. However, it is telling that such views have historically been dismissed as thinly disguised atheism by most of the religious. If God is equated with nature as generally understood, then God simply becomes a kind of honorific term, like calling the Earth Gaia. If, on the other hand, nature is supposed to have the properties of a god, such as omniscience and omnibenevolence, it is not nature as we know it at all. Religious naturalism is either a kind of atheism that advocates reverence for the natural world or else it is an attempt to ascribe to nature properties usually reserved for the supernatural.

Materialism goes one step further than basic naturalism and claims that the only things that are real are material objects, made up of atoms and sub-atomic particles. Modern science has made this view obsolete, replaced by the more sophisticated *physicalism* that holds that the world is composed not just of matter, but the fields, forces, and everything else described by physics. Although materialism is wrong, its basic premise has not been discredited. In the words of two contemporary physicalists, Robin Gordon Brown and James Ladyman, that premise is that physics is 'the most general science that concerns itself with all phenomena'. Both materialists and physicists are committed to the view that everything is made from the 'stuff' of physics; it is simply that the materialists had a mistaken view about what this stuff was.

There are strong forms of physicalism that deny the reality of much of what we take to be real and valuable. The strongest of these positions is usually called scientism, often as an insult. Scientism is the claim that the only things that really exist are the things that can be described in the physical sciences. Everything else is in some sense an illusion. Alex Rosenberg proudly defends this claim, embracing the label scientism. The title of his book *The Atheist's Guide to Reality* reinforces the common belief that all atheists are scientistic. This in turn portrays the atheist as a kind of nihilist, who not only denies the existence of God, but also the existence of anything other than physical objects.

However, atheists need not and usually do not take such a reductive view. The alternative is to accept that physics describes the fundamental structure of the universe and that from this platform other complex, non-physical phenomena can emerge, most evidently consciousness, thoughts, and emotions. You can be a naturalist and believe these things are just as real as quarks and neutrons. Indeed, to deny minds exist would seem absurd, since it takes a mind to make such a denial.

Naturalists must of course accept that minds only exist because we have functioning, embodied brains. But to understand what a mind is we have to be careful to avoid making what Gilbert Ryle termed a 'category mistake'. This mistake is to think that mind and matter both refer to substances. This has led many to conclude that there must be two different kinds of substance in my head— mental (my mind) and physical (my brain). But it has also led some naturalists to believe that the mind is a lump of *physical* stuff, just another word for brain. This is to make the same mistake. The mind is not an object. Rather mind can be seen as what the embodied brain does. So although the naturalist is committed to the view there is only one lump of stuff in my head, my brain, that does not mean the mind is the brain. This brain is what allows me to have a mind, meaning the conscious experiences and thoughts that make up my mental life.

One reason we're tricked into thinking the mind must be a thing is because the word 'mind' is a noun. But not all nouns refer to objects. Consider love. No one thinks that love is a special kind of substance. To feel love is not to touch a strange kind of object. Yet many people believe in love, feel love, give love, and so on. Love is real, but it is not a substance. If we have no problem with this thought, why do we have a problem with the idea that minds are real but are not a special kind of mental substance? Lumps of stuff are not the only real things in a physical universe.

These are philosophically deep waters which we can but dip our toes into here. For the moment, I just want to stress that the atheist need not be a crude denier of all that cannot be described by science. Most atheism is rooted not in scientism or even in the specific claims of physicalism but in the broader claims of naturalism. The natural world is home to more than can be described scientifically, such as the feel of conscious experience, beauty, emotions, moral values—in short the full gamut of phenomena that gives richness to life. Once more, the moral of the story is that the atheist denies the existence of God but is not by nature a denier full stop.

The fact that atheists almost all share a naturalistic understanding of the world does not mean that they agree on what follows from this. There is a lot of diversity within atheism about ethics, politics, and philosophy, just as there is a lot of diversity within and between religions. Still, their shared, positive conception of the nature of the universe is both sufficient and significant enough for us to put atheists together in a single category.

We are not yet done with challenging the perceived negativity of atheism. Many people believe that without God there can be no morality, no meaning to life, no human goodness. As we shall soon see, this is false. Atheism is only intrinsically negative when it comes to belief about God and the supernatural. Even then atheists can be indifferent rather than hostile. Atheists are capable of taking a positive view of many aspects of life. They can be at least as moral, sensitive to aesthetic experience, and attuned to natural beauty as theists, if not more so.

Chapter 2
The case for atheism

Absence and evidence

It is often assumed that the case for atheism is doomed from the start. Its central claim—that there is no God—is not something that can ever be proven. 'Absence of evidence is not evidence of absence.'

Things are not quite as simple, however, as this slogan makes out. Consider the question of whether there is any butter in my fridge. If we don't open the door and have a look inside there will be an absence of evidence for the butter being there, but this would not be evidence of its absence. However, if we look inside the fridge, thoroughly examine it and don't find any butter, then we have an absence of evidence which really does add up to evidence of absence. Indeed, it is hard to see what other evidence there could be for something *not* being there other than the failure to find any evidence that it *is* there.

The difference between the absence of evidence when we don't look in the fridge and the absence once we have looked is simple: the former is an absence due to a failure to look where evidence might be found; the latter is an absence due to a failure to find evidence where it would be found, if the thing being looked for actually existed. The latter kind of absence of evidence is strong evidence for absence. Think about it: the strongest evidence that, for example, there is no elephant in your fridge is that you find no signs of one when you open the fridge door.

The case for atheism does not rest purely on the failure to find evidence for God's existence anyway. As we have seen, atheism is essentially a form of naturalism. The case for atheism does not therefore depend on proving God does not exist but on making a good case for naturalism.

In order for this case to be strong it need not amount to a decisive proof. In many contexts we settle for less than absolute proof because we know it is not possible. In English criminal law, for instance, the standard of proof is 'beyond reasonable doubt'. In civil cases, however, the bar is set lower at the balance of probabilities, meaning that you only have to show your story is more likely than not to win the case.

Proof of ultimate matters is beyond all of us and given the disagreements among intelligent people, even to insist on an argument that is beyond reasonable doubt seems, well, unreasonable. The case for atheism can be made merely on the balance of probabilities. I will argue, however, that it is stronger than this, that there is what lawyers call clear and convincing evidence for the truth of atheism.

Evidence for atheism

In ordinary speech we appeal to all kinds of evidence: 'I heard it on the news,' 'I saw it with my own eyes,' 'In tests eight out of ten cats said their owners preferred it.'

The problem is, of course, that not all evidence is good evidence. One principle of quality control is that evidence is stronger if it is available to inspection by more people on repeated occasions; and worse if it is confined to the testimony of a small number of people on limited occasions.

We can see how this principle works by considering two extreme examples. The evidence that water freezes at zero degrees Celsius is an example of the best kind of evidence. In principle, anyone can test this out at any time for themselves and each test makes the evidence more compelling.

Now consider the other extreme: the testimony of a single person relating one incident. Someone claims that they saw their dog spontaneously combust right before their very eyes. Is this good evidence for the existence of spontaneous canine combustion? Not at all, for various reasons. First, as the Scottish philosopher David Hume pointed out, this solitary testimony has to be balanced against the much larger amount of evidence that dogs don't just burst into flames. Hume's point is not that the testimony of this one person isn't evidence at all. It is rather that it is insignificant when we compare it to all the other evidence we have that spontaneous canine combustion does not take place.

A second reason why it is not good evidence is that human beings are not very good at interpreting their experiences, especially unusual ones. Take as a simple example the experience of seeing an illusionist who pretends to have real powers bending a metal spoon without apparently exerting any physical force. People persuaded by such experiments say that they 'saw the person bend the spoon with their thoughts'. Of course they saw no such thing, not least because they could not see the illusionist's thoughts, which means they couldn't have seen the thoughts bend the metal. What they saw was a spoon bending while not seeing any physical force being exerted on it, that's all. Everything else is interpretation.

To say this is not to call the witness a liar or a fool. They are neither. They did not lie, they were just mistaken; they are not fools, but victims of clever tricksters. They should have been more sceptical because of Hume's principle: any evidence for psychokinesis should have been outweighed by the evidence of all their other experiences to date. This scepticism is vindicated by the fact that when the spoon benders are tested in laboratory conditions, none is able to replicate the feat. Just as evidence becomes stronger when it is available to inspection by more people on repeated occasions, it is weaker when it disappears altogether when it is inspected at all.

What I want to suggest is that all the strong evidence tells in favour of naturalism, and therefore almost all kinds of atheism, and only weak evidence tells against it.

Consider one of the biggest questions where the evidence has something to contribute: the nature of persons. The atheist's naturalism consists in the view that a human being is a biological animal rather than some kind of embodied spiritual soul, as many religious believers think. The strong evidence all points to our biological nature. For example, consciousness remains in many ways a mystery. But all we do know about it shows that it is a product of brain activity and that with no brain, there is no consciousness. In fact, this is so startlingly obvious that it is astonishing that anyone can really doubt it. The data of neuroscience show that all the diverse experiences which we associate with consciousness depend on particular processes in the brain and body. If you inhibit or damage an area of the brain that is necessary for a particular form of conscious activity, that conscious activity will cease, except in those cases where another part of the brain can take over the job. (More bizarrely, if you stimulate certain areas of the brain you can sometimes induce involuntary conscious activity. For instance, by stimulating the area of the brain associated with humour, you can make someone find anything hilarious.) And although we cannot look into the minds of others, when their brains cease functioning they certainly stop displaying all the signs of conscious life.

If any one thing distinguishes us as individual persons then that must be our capacity for consciousness and rational thought. And if this capacity is entirely dependent on our organic brains, as the strong evidence suggests, then the atheist view that we are mortal, biological organisms is strongly supported.

The counter-evidence that consciousness can continue beyond the death of the brain is extremely weak. It can almost all be put into two categories: out of body experiences (OBEs) such as those that occur near death, and supposed communication with the dead, directly or via some kind of medium.

There are countless spooky stories about both kinds of experiences which seem to refute naturalism. Take the case of the neurosurgeon Eben Alexander who had an OBE and subsequently studied his own medical charts. He concluded that 'My entire neocortex—the outer surface of the brain, the part that makes us human—was entirely shut down.' In other words, 'During my coma my brain wasn't working improperly—It wasn't working *at all*.' The only explanation he had for his experience was that his soul had left his body. As the title of his book *Proof of Heaven* shows, he considers the evidence decisive and talks about the 'knowledge' he has acquired about our true nature.

It is evident that many people have these and other spiritual experiences and that they can be profoundly meaningful. Typically, as Alexander himself found, there is a deep sense that the 'universe of separate objects turns out to be a complete illusion' and that 'every object in the physical universe is intimately connected with every other object'. This is not perceived as something merely felt but as a genuine insight, a factual discovery.

Such testimonies can be multiplied seemingly without limit. Similarly, the sceptical naturalist will be asked, what about the medium who led people to the body of a murdered child, using information no one living could possibly have? Why do the police use mediums if they are unreliable? How do you explain how the medium told the widow something only her dead husband could possibly have known?

However, 'whataboutism' is not a good argument. The demand that the atheist provide a case-by-case rebuttal of all alleged cases of consciousness without a body is unfair. It is just impossible for anyone to assess all the individual claims that are made. But we don't need to. As the statistician's adage puts it, the plural of anecdote is not data. The multiplication of cases is only a multiplication of evidence if each individual item actually is good evidence.

This is not the case. All the evidence for life after death is of the weak variety. It is anecdotal, meaning that it relies heavily or entirely on personal testimony without checks and verifications. OBEs are very powerful but they only report what people *remember* how things *seemed* to them, once they have regained consciousness. Time and again you find that claims that people saw things they could not have seen from their bodies turn out to be unverified. At the moment, the best explanation for OBEs comes from a Swiss neuroscientist Olaf Blanke, who says they are 'related to a failure to integrate multisensory information from one's own body at the temporo-parietal junction (TPJ)'.

Neither have so-called cases of communication with the dead left us with anything approaching the kind of generally observable, verifiable data that is characteristic of strong evidence. So the question for the non-atheist must be, why do they think that a few pieces of such weak evidence for life after death will suffice to outweigh the mountain of strong evidence for the mortality of human consciousness?

If the evidence for disembodied consciousness were of the strong variety, its relative rareness might not matter. If, for instance, there were one ghost who could reliably and repeatedly talk to living humans, observed by others, that single survival of death alone would be enough to make the atheist reconsider their belief in human mortality. But none of the evidence for disembodied human existence even approaches this strength. Indeed, on closer inspection, almost all of these alleged pieces of evidence turn out to be much weaker than they at first seem and not a single one has proven to be decisive. No medium has ever been able to tell us something that proves beyond reasonable doubt that they are party to information from the 'spirit world'. Despite what you may have heard, no one has ever come to know something during an OBE that they could not possibly have known if they had not actually left their body. Nor do the police use clairvoyance in their investigations.

Even the rare examples of genuinely puzzling evidence for life after death should not trouble the naturalist. Let us say that in one instance (or maybe even a dozen), a medium has said something only the dead could know. The point is still that such rare, unrepeatable pieces of weak evidence are outweighed by the mass of strong evidence for the mortality of the self. Remember also that every day millions of reports are made by mediums. By pure luck alone a few are bound to be uncanny. It would be foolish to consider individual examples of such 'communications' greater evidence than all we know about human mortality.

It smacks of wishful thinking and self-delusion when people are prepared to place more importance on anecdotal weak evidence than they are on strong evidence for our mortality. As David Hume pointed out, we have a natural tendency to be bewitched by wonder and mystery, which gives us a strong desire to believe tales of the extraordinary. The atheist can justly say that, when time and again the evidence for supernatural events is not as it first seems, they are justified in assuming all similar cases to be equally weak unless proven otherwise. Hence the onus is on the non-atheist, not to demand an explanation from the atheist, but to make a case that a tale of disembodied existence is more than just a repetition of hearsay.

However, arguments for our mortality seem powerless in the face of a strong belief in or desire for life after death. Just as the person with an obsessive-compulsive disorder can never be sure they have actually locked the door no matter how many times they go back to check, so the person who thinks there may be life after death can never be sure that the possibility has been ruled out for good, no matter how many times they review the evidence. The logical possibility always remains that the piece of 'killer evidence' will emerge that we are not mortal after all. This permanent possibility can sustain hope and belief.

The problem is that such permanent possibilities exist for almost all beliefs. It is possible, for instance, that tomorrow it will be revealed that you have lived all your life in a virtual reality machine; that aliens have been preparing for an invasion of earth for the last hundred years; that the Pope is a robot; that the Apollo mission never made it to the Moon and the whole landing was filmed in a studio; that the evangelical Christians were right all along and judgement day has arrived. But the mere possibility that such things might be true is no reason to believe them. Indeed, the fact that the evidence to date suggests strongly they are not true is good reason to disbelieve them.

Why uncertainty is inevitable

Whenever we reach conclusions based on the evidence of past experience, some residual uncertainty is inevitable. This is an in-built feature of *induction*: arguing from what has been observed in the past or present to reach conclusions about what hasn't been observed, in the past, present, or future. This is the only reliable method we have for drawing conclusions about how the world is and how it works.

Induction is premised on the uniformity of nature—the idea that the laws of nature do not suddenly suspend themselves or change. Note that this is not the same as saying that nature is always *predictable*. Many natural events are extremely unpredictable. But none of this unpredictable behaviour breaks natural laws. Freak weather is not uncaused weather.

We all of us, theist and atheist, make this assumption about the uniformity of nature, every minute of the day. Even if you are just sitting down doing nothing, you relax on the assumption that gravity is not about to stop keeping you sitting down, that the material the chair is made of will not suddenly turn to liquid, or that the tea you are drinking won't suddenly poison you. But our reliance on the principle is not supported by strict logic. From the premise 'This is how things have always been when observed' it does not logically follow that 'This is how things always have been, are, and will be.' Hence the child who believes their toys come to life when they go to sleep but never when they are awake is not making a *logical* error: no truths about what they observe when they are awake can ever provide enough evidence for a logical proof that the same happens when they are asleep.

Nevertheless, we do believe the child is mistaken. We do so because we depend entirely on inductive forms of argument to make sense of the world around us. Atheists can argue that, if we apply this inductive method consistently, their own case is further supported. The evidence of experience is that we live in a world governed by natural laws, that everything that happens in it is explained by natural phenomena. It is true that some things remain unexplained, but the atheist can argue that when a good explanation finally does come along, that explanation is always naturalistic. Experience shows us that to be explained just is to be explained in naturalistic terms. The class of unexplained phenomena therefore is unlikely to contain anything supernatural.

If we accept the inductive method, which we must, to be consistent we must also accept that it points towards a naturalism that supports atheism, not any kind of supernaturalism that supports theism. The fact that inductive arguments do not give us absolute certainty is a brute fact we have to live with. We have to live with the uncertainty of induction in order to function in the world at all.

Arguments to the best explanation

There is a second type of argument which is based on evidence but which does not admit of strict proof: abduction. Abduction is also known by its more descriptive name, argument to the best explanation. An abductive argument examines a phenomenon or set of phenomena that has more than one possible explanation and attempts to determine which of these explanations is most likely to be true.

Abductive reasoning is not entirely separable from induction. In assessing probabilities, we have to draw on inductive inferences about how the world tends to behave. Candidates for the best explanation for why the door is open, for example, will not include the possibility that the room wanted a bit of air. There is also a sense in which abduction underpins induction: the hypothesis that the uniformity we observe in nature reflects a genuine uniformity is more plausible than one that assumes nature works differently when we're not looking.

There is no formula for determining which explanation is the best, but in general better explanations are simpler, more coherent, and more comprehensive than the alternatives. They are also likely to be testable in some way or have some predictive power.

Like inductive arguments, adductive ones cannot be conclusive: it always remains possible that the least likely explanation turns out to be the true one. But also like induction, abduction is something we cannot do without. If it fails to guarantee us a true conclusion, that is a fact we just have to live with.

When it comes to the nature of the universe, there are many explanations for the way the world is as it appears to be, and since these explanations are in conflict with each other, not all of them can be true. It is wishful thinking to suppose that one or another could be proven to be the true one. To borrow a phrase from Derrida, 'If things were simple word would have got around.' So we can do no better than survey the options and decide which explanation fits the facts better. If we do this, we see that the naturalistic atheist understanding provides the best explanation.

First, atheism is simpler than the alternatives in that it only requires us to posit the existence of one, natural world. To add to this an unobserved supernatural world is not only metaphysically extravagant, it is also untestable, since the supernatural world is by definition unobservable.

The naturalism of the atheist is also more coherent, because it has everything in the universe fitting into one scheme of being. Those who posit a supernatural realm have to explain how it interacts and coexists with the natural one. Such a two-realm view is by its nature more fragmented than the unified one of the atheist.

Atheism also has great explanatory power when it comes to the existence of divergent religious beliefs. The best explanation for the fact that different religious people believe different things about God and the universe throughout the world is that religion is a human construct that does not correspond to any independent metaphysical reality. The alternative is that many religions exist but only one (or a few) are true. It's no good saying that all religions are different paths to the same truth: religions often flatly contradict each other and if we were to focus simply on what all religions agree on, we would be left with very little indeed.

Hindus and Christians are not worshipping the same God, not least because Hindus themselves differ in how they conceive of God and gods. Christians and Muslims fundamentally disagree in that the former see Christ as the messiah and the latter do not. Given the centrality of Christ to the Christian faith, it requires a lot of fudging of doctrine to insist that Islam and Christianity are both really true.

One can make the comparison of whether naturalism or supernaturalism offers the best explanation with specific issues. What best explains the existence of evil in the world? You can choose between the atheist hypothesis that, as evolved creatures, there should be no expectation that the world should be an entirely good place, or the religious explanation that requires rather a lot of sophistical reasoning to reconcile belief in an all-powerful, all-loving designer God and all the terrible and pointless suffering and injustice in his creation.

What best explains the strength of the sex drive? You can choose between the hypothesis that natural selection favoured it over a weaker one and the hypothesis that God made us randy in a perverse attempt to make us more likely to sin.

Time and time again, I suggest, the better explanation for the way the world is and appears to be is that it is a natural phenomenon. Even though such explanations may not be complete, explanations that bring in supernatural elements are much less plausible and at times simply preposterous.

Atheism and agnosticism

Atheism contrasts not only with theism and other forms of belief in God, but also with agnosticism—the suspension of belief or disbelief in God. The agnostic claims we cannot know whether God exists and so the only rational option is to reserve judgement. For the agnostic, both the theist and the atheist go too far in affirming or denying God's existence—we just don't have sufficient evidence or arguments to justify either position.

It is widely believed that while agnosticism is intellectually respectable, atheism goes too far, not just when it comes to God. For instance, many people say that, since the atheist can never know for sure that there is no life after death, it is foolish for them to believe there is none. At best they should suspend belief and be agnostic. (It is also interesting to note that many of the people who claim that atheists should be agnostics are religious believers. Surely if they were consistent they should become agnostics themselves?)

The idea that atheism goes too far might seem to have been the view of David Hume, the 18th-century Scottish philosopher known as 'the great infidel' and a hero to many atheists today (Figure 1).

1. **David Hume by Allan Ramsay (1766).**

Denis Diderot recounts a story of Hume at a dinner hosted by the openly atheist Baron D'Holbach. Hume reportedly said that he did not believe in atheists, because he had never seen one. The Baron told him that of the eighteen around the table, fifteen were atheists and 'the three others haven't made up their minds'.

However, to say Hume was an agnostic would also be misleading, given how the term is generally used and understood. Hume would not go so far as to say that God *definitely* did not exist, and in that sense was agnostic. But he clearly considered it a possibility that could and should be set aside as far too improbable to merit concern, and in that sense did not suspend judgement and so was not agnostic. This was the view of another atheist icon, Bertrand Russell (see Figure 2), who in an essay entitled 'Am I an Atheist or an Agnostic?' wrote:

2. Bertrand Russell in 1957.

As a philosopher, if I were speaking to a purely philosophic audience I should say that I ought to describe myself as an Agnostic, because I do not think that there is a conclusive argument by which one can prove that there is not a God.

On the other hand, if I am to convey the right impression to the ordinary man in the street I think I ought to say that I am an Atheist, because when I say that I cannot prove that there is not a God, I ought to add equally that I cannot prove that there are not the Homeric gods.

To call someone an agnostic would suggest that they had suspended judgement on God's existence, not that they thought it as unlikely as the existence of Hermes the winged messenger.

Should we then consider Hume and Russell to be atheists only in a weak sense? I don't think so. A sceptical alternative to the dogmatism of the French *philosophes* that Hume found objectionable is not shoulder-shrugging agnosticism but an atheism that is not dogmatic. 'Firmly held belief' is not the same as dogmatism, even though the two are often confused. At the heart of the distinction is the technical term 'defeasibility'. Beliefs or truth claims are said to be *defeasible* when the possibility remains open that they could be shown to be wrong. Beliefs or truth claims that are *indefeasible* are hence ones for which there is no possibility of their being disproven.

To be dogmatic is to hold that one's beliefs are indefeasible when such a refusal to countenance the possibility of being wrong is not justified. A dogmatic atheist is therefore someone who holds that God does not exist and that there is no way that their belief could possibly be wrong. A dogmatic theist is similarly someone who holds that God exists and that there is no way that their belief could possibly be wrong. It would be fair to object to both these dogmatists that their beliefs are unjustified, since there is no way either can be so sure that they are right.

But this does not mean that they should become agnostics. All it means is that they should allow for the defeasibility of their beliefs, to admit it is possible that they could be wrong. This is not agnosticism. Indeed, one can have *very strongly* held beliefs and still admit their defeasibility. For instance, an atheist might say that they believe there are no good reasons for being anything other than an atheist and that they themselves cannot seriously imagine that they are wrong. But just as long as they are open to the possibility that they could be wrong they are not dogmatic. Of course, this openness is only genuine if one sincerely accepts this possibility and doesn't just gesture towards it. As long as that sincerity is there, there is no reason why one cannot have firmly held atheist beliefs and thus follow the middle path between unwarranted agnosticism and dogmatism.

Why is this middle path so often missed? I think it is part of a collective myth, which owes its origins to philosophers such as Plato, that there is a sharp distinction between knowledge, which is absolutely certain, and opinion, which isn't. It is too easily assumed that the mere introduction of grounds for doubt is enough to warrant the suspension of our beliefs. But this maxim cannot be followed. We cannot be absolutely sure of anything, save perhaps for the fact of our own existence (and even then only at the time we are aware of it). So if we are not justified in firmly believing anything we are not sure of, we would have to suspend belief about everything.

This is not the right moral to draw from the truism that absolute certainty is elusive. It does not follow from the fact that we could be wrong that we have no good reasons to think we are right. Who seriously claims we should say, 'I neither believe nor disbelieve that the Pope is a robot' or 'As to whether or not eating this piece of chocolate will turn me into an elephant I am completely agnostic'? In the absence of any good reasons to believe the outlandish claims, we rightly disbelieve them, we don't just suspend judgement.

Uncertainty does not require agnosticism, but it does suggest we should not hold our views too tightly. This applies even to the most basic atheist commitment to naturalism. Just as Hume was in a narrow, technical sense an agnostic about God, he was also probably similarly agnostic about naturalism. In his *Dialogues Concerning Natural Religion*, the character usually supposed to be his mouthpiece, Philo, asks rhetorically, 'A very small part of this great system, during a very short time, is very imperfectly discovered to us: and do we thence pronounce decisively concerning the origin of the whole?' We cannot claim to know for sure the ultimate nature of the universe. But since the strongest evidence points towards naturalism, it makes sense to live on the strong and justified assumption that it is the right view.

I am as opposed to dogmatic atheism as anyone, and I am also opposed to dogmatic theism. Indeed, it is my personal view that the holding of dogmatic views of any kind is in general more dangerous than the views themselves. Thoughtful atheists often have much more in common with undogmatic theists than one might suppose.

Is atheism a faith position?

When religious critics claim that atheism is a faith position they intend to cut it down to size, not to flatter it. This is strange since traditionally faith has been something special that believers have and non-believers—the faithless—lack. To make faith a great leveller shows a loss of faith in the power of faith.

What's more, if the requirement for faith puts all belief systems on the same level, we would seem to be left with a kind of relativism: you have your faith, I have mine, and neither of us can criticize the other for being more or less reasonable.

This is particularly odd for Christians since one of the most repeated Gospel verses is 'I am the way, the truth and the life.

No one comes to the father except through me' (John 14:6). Jesus is not reported to have said, 'I am *one* way, *one* truth and *one* life. People can come to the father whatever way they want.' Nor did he reportedly finish his speech by saying, 'But that's just what I believe—your faith may be different.'

With few exceptions, however, atheism just isn't a faith position. To see why, we need to ask just what makes something a matter of faith rather than reason.

When people argue that atheism is a faith position, they tend to say that, since there is no proof for atheism, something extra—faith—is required to justify belief in it. But as we have seen, it just isn't the case that we always need faith to bridge the gap between 100 per cent proof and belief. Where we have a lack of absolute proof we can still have overwhelming evidence or one explanation which is far superior to the alternatives. When such grounds for belief are available we have no need for faith. It is not faith that justifies my belief that eating fresh fruit and vegetables is good for me, but evidence. Nor do I need faith to take tried and tested medications. In neither case, however, can I be completely sure that the nutritional or medical advice is correct.

If we say that faith is required to commit to *any* belief or action that is not strictly proven, then there is nothing to distinguish faith from ordinary belief. Everything becomes a matter of faith, except for perhaps belief in a few self-evident truths such as $1 + 1 = 2$. Faith is robbed of its distinctive character.

If we did expand the scope of faith to cover all belief, we'd still have to accept that there are *degrees* of faith. It clearly takes less faith to believe in the refreshing power of water than it does the healing power of Christ. But to then say that the beliefs of atheists are '*just* a matter of faith' would be an empty objection. If everything is a matter of faith, this is a trivial fact. To make it non-trivial the beliefs of atheists would have to require *at least as much* faith as those of religious believers. But they don't, because the atheist position is based on evidence and argument. The atheist believes in what she has good reason to believe in and doesn't believe in anything where there are only few or weak reasons to do so. If this is a faith position then the amount of faith required is extremely small.

Contrast this with believers in the supernatural and we can see what a true faith position is. Belief in the supernatural is belief in the absence of strong evidence. Indeed, sometimes it is belief in something which is *contrary* to the available evidence. Belief in life after death, for example, is contrary to the wealth of evidence we have that people are mortal animals.

This shows where I believe the real fault line between faith positions and ordinary beliefs lies. It is not about *proof*, but about distinguishing between beliefs which are in accord with evidence, experience, or logic and those which lack or are contrary to evidence, experience, or logic. Atheism is not a faith position because it is belief in nothing beyond that which is supported by evidence and argument. Religious belief is a faith position because it goes beyond what there is evidence or argument for. That is why faith requires something 'special' that ordinary belief does not have.

This interpretation of faith accords with the message of the two great Christian parables of faith, the stories of Abraham and doubting Thomas. Thomas was one of Jesus' disciples and he famously refused to believe that Jesus had risen from the dead, as some of Jesus' other followers had claimed. Note that he did not need to have faith to believe that Jesus had died. Rather he lacked faith that Jesus had risen from the dead. The asymmetry is due to the fact that it requires no faith to believe in that to which all the evidence points, but it does require faith to believe in something which flies in the face of experience and evidence. Thomas only believes when he is shown Jesus and told to place his hands in his

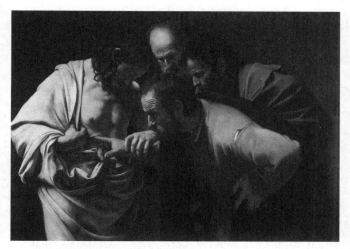

3. Caravaggio, *Doubting Thomas*, c.1600.

wounds. The moral of the story is that 'blessed are those who have not seen and yet have believed' (John 20:29). Thus Christianity endorsed the principle that it is good to believe what you have no evidence to believe, a rather convenient maxim for a belief system unsupported by good evidence (see Figure 3).

Abraham was asked to sacrifice his only son to God, in order to test his faith. In Kierkegaard's penetrating analysis of this story, the reason this is such a great test of faith is not because it is a test of obedience. After all, if God tells you to do something, he must have good reasons, and if you truly believe, you know that you and your son will be safe in the long run. Rather, it is a test of faith because it flies in the face of everything Abraham knows about God, morality, and goodness. Reason and experience all point to the fact that God would never command such a human sacrifice. And yet it seems he has done so. Is Abraham deluded? Is God trying to test him a different way—is he supposed to defy the order and so prove his goodness? Or is it not God asking him at all, but

27

the devil? Abraham requires faith to go ahead because what he is asked to do defies reason.

The status of atheist and religious belief are thus quite different. Only religious belief requires faith because only religion requires us to believe in the absence of good evidence. It is a simple error to suppose that just because atheist beliefs are also 'unproven' or 'uncertain' that they too require faith. There may be some atheists whose belief in the inevitability of progress or the power of science, for instance, goes far beyond what evidence suggests. Such people may be said to have faith in science or in progress. But atheism itself does not necessarily or typically rest on faith. Faith is not needed to plug any gap, however small, between having non-conclusive reasons to believe and certain proof. Rather faith supports beliefs which lack the ordinary support of evidence or argument. And that is why, as the traditional religious texts tell us, faith is not as easy as ordinary belief.

Arguing for God

Pick up any introduction to the philosophy of religion and you'll see a number of traditional arguments for the existence of God. If any of these worked, they would obviously be fatal counter-arguments to atheism. Despite the volumes devoted to them, and the innumerable versions that have been proposed over the years, each has a basic core structure which makes it clear why they fail.

One of the worst is the *cosmological argument*, which is that since everything must have a cause, the universe must have a cause. And the only cause that could be up to the job is God, or at least, God is the best hypothesis. The cosmological argument is implied whenever someone turns around and says to the naturalist, 'Ah, well the universe may have begun with the big bang, but what caused the big bang?'

The argument is to my mind utterly awful, a disgrace to the good name of philosophy. One fatal flaw among many is that the argument is based on a premise that it then flouts: that nothing exists uncaused and that the cause of something great and complex must be itself even greater and more complex. But it ends by hypothesizing God's existence as simple and uncaused. But if it is possible for God to exist without a cause greater than God, why can't the universe exist without a cause greater than itself? Either everything needs a cause greater than itself or it doesn't.

The second fatal flaw is that even if the logic of the argument works, we do not arrive at God. What we arrive at is a cause which is greater and more complex than the universe itself and which is itself uncaused. Whether or not this resembles the traditional God, who is much more like a super-person than a super-universe, is surely open to question. So the argument cannot really establish that the cause of the universe is anything like God at all (see Figure 4).

The teleological argument is another terrible piece of reasoning. It compares the universe to a mechanism such as a watch. If you find a watch you have to suppose that there was a watchmaker. Such a complex, intricate mechanism could not have come into existence by pure chance. Now consider the universe: it is even more intricate and complex and so there is even more reason to suppose it did not come into existence by chance. Therefore, there must be some great architect or designer behind it: God.

The analogy fails because the universe just isn't a mechanism like a watch. When we see a rabbit, for example, we do not look for a rabbit maker. We think instead it had parents. Unlike artefacts, objects in the natural world emerge through natural processes which are well understood. Read a book like Richard Dawkins's *The Blind Watchmaker*, for example, and you can see how evolution accounts for the appearance of design we find. Indeed, if you look at what we do know about how universes form and

4. **Anonymous, God as the architect of the universe, *c.*1220–30.**

organisms grow, the hand of any designer is conspicuous only by its absence.

Furthermore, as David Hume pointed out, we can only hypothesize a watchmaker because we know by experience what the causes of watches are. We have no such experience of causes of the universe, so we are not justified in making any assumptions about who or what it might be.

The cosmological and teleological arguments are examples of the perennial temptation to hypothesize a 'God of the gaps', where God is used to explain what we cannot currently explain. This is a risky strategy. After all, people previously invoked God to explain all sorts of natural phenomena we later explained, and each time God had to retreat further back into the unknown. Today God is often found retreating to lighting the blue touch-paper that started the universe going or fine-tuning its fundamental forces. Such a God is fast running out of places of refuge.

The religious have other reasons to avoid seeing their God as a cosmic hole filler. In the 19th century, Henry Drummond argued that 'an immanent God, which is the God of Evolution, is infinitely grander than the occasional wonder-worker, who is the God of an old theology'. If you believe in God, is it not better to believe in one who is big enough to be everywhere, not one who is confined to doing the leftover tasks his creation cannot manage for itself?

The last of the terrible trio of classic arguments is the *ontological argument*, which is at least philosophically interesting. It is an attempt to show that some kind of logical contradiction is generated if we suppose that God does not exist, and that therefore God by logical necessity must exist. For instance, the concept of God is of a supremely perfect entity. A perfect entity that did not exist would clearly not be supremely perfect, since an entity which is the same but existent would be superior. So the concept of a supremely perfect entity must be a concept of an existing entity. Therefore by examining the concept of God alone we can see that God must exist by pain of contradiction.

The way I have summarized this argument makes its flaw clear: all we can show by logic is that the *concept* of God includes the *concept* of existence. But these are merely truths about concepts. We cannot jump from such truths about concepts to reach conclusions about what exists in the real world. For example, the concept of a circle is clearly defined by mathematical formulae, but we cannot conclude from the concept of a circle that any actual circles that meet the strict mathematical formulation exist in the real world, or even that real space conforms to the rules of Euclidean geometry within which circles are defined.

Many pairs of concepts logically require each other without proving that they refer to anything that actually exists. For instance, a wife without a husband cannot exist and still be a wife. But the woman who is the wife could exist without a husband, it's just that she would no longer be a wife. Continue the analogy with God and existence and you do not get the stunning conclusion that God must exist, but the banal truth that a God without existence could not exist. It's not that God must exist, but that *if* God exists, God must exist.

The main purpose of having some familiarity with these arguments is that versions of them are still sometimes wheeled out by religious believers to challenge the atheist. The fact that they fail so spectacularly, however, is not an argument against religion. Indeed, the arguments rarely explain why people become religious. Many believers agree with Peter Vardy, a Christian philosopher and author of several leading textbooks in the philosophy of religion, who considers the traditional arguments to be 'a waste of time'.

The most that some of these arguments can do is to serve as *apologetics*. Apologetics is the attempt to show that belief is *compatible* with reason, not that reason *leads to* belief. Take as an analogy parents whose child has gone missing and the most likely explanation is that she is dead. They may persist with the belief that their child is still alive. They can't provide any arguments that prove this, or even make it more likely than not, but as long as no body has been found they can explain why their belief is not inconsistent with the facts.

Apologetics works in the same way. There is no way to prove that God exists. But when our scientific worldview has no place for God and so many arguments point to a naturalistic universe, believers want to have arguments to show that they are not simply being irrational. Like Kant, their project is to 'abolish knowledge', meaning certainty, 'to make room for faith'.

The real grounds of faith

One of the most interesting contemporary apologists is Alvin Plantinga. He argues that the fundamental grounding of anyone's belief has to be something that cannot be proven. Even a scientist has to assume their own sanity, the reliability of experimental data, and the uniformity of nature. Such beliefs are 'properly basic', meaning that they are the beliefs that all others rest on, we cannot do without them, and we are justified in having them. On this, most philosophers would agree. But Plantinga argues that experience of encountering the divine justifies belief in God as properly basic. Faith is 'a special source of knowledge, knowledge that can't be arrived at by way of reason alone'.

Whatever we make of Plantinga's argument, it's important to recognize that for the vast majority of believers, God's existence is not a hypothesis like any other, to be settled by careful weighing of reason and arguments. Their faith is rooted in something more immediate, even visceral. For instance, Russell Stannard is a leading physicist who wrote a book called *The God Experiment* on the evidence for God's existence. But when pushed by an interviewer he said, 'I don't have to believe in God, I *know* that God exists—that is how I feel.' In other words, evidence and arguments are neither here nor there—it is his personal conviction that really counts.

When personal experience and conviction is indeed the ground of religious belief, it is disingenuous for believers to put forward arguments to support their beliefs. Similarly, it is futile for atheists to attack the religious with arguments undermining these reasons for belief if they are not genuine reasons for belief at all.

To place personal conviction at the heart of belief should not, however, put an end to all reasoned debate. First, we should be very careful about what we say cannot be doubted. 'Cannot be doubted' can really mean 'don't want to doubt' or 'cannot imagine the thing being doubted not being true'. It may seem to the religious that they can no more doubt God's existence than their own, but this cannot be universally true, since plenty of people lose their belief in God and yet no psychologically healthy person loses her belief in herself. (Although plenty, after philosophical reflection, lose their belief in what they thought the self was.) To those who say they cannot imagine the possibility of God not existing I say: try a little harder. Imagine what it is like for atheists. You must be able to see that they can not only live, but live with purpose and values. Try to imagine what it is like for such a person to live without God and then try to imagine yourself living such a life.

A second point is to have the honesty to recognize that reliance on faith—an inner conviction which is not based on reason or evidence but is seen as a source of knowledge—is a risky strategy. Around the world people have the same kind of conviction but with very different specific content. As an extreme example, people have felt convinced that God was calling them to do acts such as those like the 9/11 attacks. On a more everyday level, people tend to understand the divine presence they feel in terms of the image of God presented to them by their local religion. People in Muslim countries, for instance, do not feel the presence of Jesus. Indeed, even within Christian cultures, what people report to know the existence of changes over time and across denominations.

The mere fact that people use the same grounds—personal conviction—to justify belief in different, incompatible religions is enough to show that such convictions cannot be the proper basis for religious belief. This is because these convictions support all religions equally, yet not all can be true. Anything that can be used to justify numerous incompatible beliefs cannot be a secure ground for belief. Relying on one's personal convictions when there is clear evidence that such convictions are not a reliable source of knowledge is to say the least risky, if not plain rash. This is why even some theologians talk about the 'risk of faith'. Faith is indeed a risk because it runs counter to the kinds of reason and evidence that are reliable, relying instead on reasons and evidence of inner convictions that are unreliable.

The power of reason against religious belief is limited. One can make a strong case against religious belief and show how the traditional arguments for God's existence are hollow. One can even explain how belief often rests on personal convictions which are an unreliable source of knowledge. But believers often do not accept the founding assumptions of such arguments. They are starting from somewhere else: a conviction that God exists that is even stronger than the scientist's or logician's belief in their first principles. This conviction trumps all reason. So to try to defeat it by the use of reason is like trying to cut water with an axe.

Place your bets

One of the most curious arguments for religious belief is Pascal's wager. The wager starts with the supposition that we cannot be sure whether God exists or not. It concludes that in such a position of uncertainty, it is better to believe than not, since the risks of non-belief (eternal damnation, fear of death) are greater than the risks of belief (wasting some of our time being devout); and the potential rewards of belief (eternal life) are greater than those of non-belief (fewer moral constraints on this earth, with dubious benefit).

The wager is rigged because no probabilities are attached to the various outcomes. Most atheists would judge that the chances that there is a God who would condemn us to hell if we refuse to worship him are so small that it is not worth taking the bet of believing in him. But perhaps a greater problem is that, with so many religions in the world, the bet still doesn't tell us which religion to follow. Indeed, if God is so jealous and petty that he only gives eternal life to those who believe in him, might he not be more angry with those who worship in the wrong way than with those who don't worship at all?

Replay Pascal's wager fairly and it actually becomes an argument for atheism (although hardly the best one). Let us admit the possibility that a good, all-knowing, all-loving God exists, as a non-dogmatic atheist should. The odds are vanishingly small that such a God would send people to hell. We know that most people who do terrible things are damaged individuals, often with terrible childhoods. Sending them to hell would seem to be cruel and unjust. A loving God would surely reform them, something not best achieved by torture, as penal reformers constantly point out. So our fear of hell should be pretty small. Even if God were inclined to dole out post-mortem punishment it is more likely to be for the wicked than for the sceptical. So the best bet would be to act well.

What about worship? It does seem odd to suggest that the supreme being demands that we little people worship him. After all, God isn't insecure, is he? And with all the different religions available, it is hard to see how we could make an informed choice about the best way to worship anyway. So the best bet is not to worship.

What about belief in him? If God exists, then he gave us our intelligence. If we use this intelligence to conclude that he doesn't exist, it would be a bit rich of him to turn around and chastise us. We could rightly plead, as Bertrand Russell supposedly said he would, 'Why did you not give me better evidence?' Surely God would not penalize anyone for doing their best with the meagre intellectual instrument he gave them?

So, if God does exist, the most likely scenario is that he cares most about our goodness, would help to reform us if we were bad, and would be big enough to not really care if we don't worship him or believe in him. So if we want to make a bet as insurance against the possibility of God's existence, then we should be good, and the rest doesn't really matter. Atheist, agnostic, or believer, it is hard to see why an omnipotent deity would favour some over the others, and we risk making a mistake if we opt for one specific kind of religious doctrine over another. The conclusion of the wager should thus be no more than 'be good'. Atheists are well poised to follow it, as we shall see in Chapter 3.

To sum up, atheism is in almost all cases naturalism, the position which is best supported by the evidence and the one which offers the best overall explanation for why the world is at it is. In contrast to faith positions, it does not require us to believe in anything which goes beyond reason or evidence, or indeed in anything which is contrary to them. The fact that we cannot be 100 per cent certain that atheism is true is only grounds for not being dogmatic in our beliefs. It is not a reason to be agnostic, nor to believe that atheism is a faith position just like religious belief.

Still, two major questions remain unanswered at this stage. One concerns morality. If atheism is true, then what of right and wrong? The second concerns meaning or purpose. Atheism may explain a lot, but surely it cannot explain what the meaning and purpose of life is. And if this is unexplained, atheism cannot be the best explanation of the human situation. I will address both these concerns in Chapters 3 and 4.

But even if atheism did mean the end of ethics and that there is no purpose to human life, that would not be an argument against atheism's truth. It may just be that the most honest and accurate account of the world we live in reveals that morality and meaning in life are no more than wishful thinking. Fortunately, as I will go on to show, that is not the case. But in order to think about these issues clearly, we at least have to acknowledge the possibility that there is a mismatch between what we want to be true and what is true.

Chapter 3
Atheist ethics

Laws and lawgivers

Dostoevsky's Ivan Karamazov may have said, 'Without God, anything is permitted,' but I bet he never tried parking in central London on a Saturday afternoon.

This chapter is all about the truths that lie behind this joke, concerning the status of moral law and the idea that divine authority is required to uphold it. I will argue that Karamazov was wrong. Morality is more than possible without God, it is entirely independent of him. That means atheists are not only capable of leading moral lives, they may even be more able to do so than those who confuse divine law and punishment with right and wrong.

To begin with we need to consider why so many people think God is necessary for morality. One argument is that in order for there to be any law there has to be a lawgiver, and ultimately, a judge. Divine law needs the equivalent of a legislature to make law and a judiciary to uphold it. Only God can fulfil both these roles (see Figure 5).

This argument confuses two separate things—law and morality. Law certainly does require a legislature and judiciary. But having these in place does not guarantee that the laws enacted and

5. Hieronymus Bosch, *The Last Judgement*, c.1482–1516.

enforced will be just and good. One can have immoral laws as well as moral ones. That is why civil disobedience can be morally justified. People who defied South Africa's apartheid laws, for instance, were behaving illegally *and* morally. Morality is thus separate from law. It is the basis upon which just laws are enacted and enforced; it is not constituted by the laws themselves.

If we see God as the divine lawmaker, we would therefore still have to ask the question: what is it that guarantees the moral laws God enacts and enforces are indeed good? The traditional answer is because God *is* good, and therefore obviously only decrees good laws. The righteousness of the moral law does not depend on God's status as a lawmaker and enforcer but on his moral goodness.

But as Plato convincingly argued over two millennia ago, this means that goodness rather than godness forms the basis of morality. In a dialogue called *Euthyphro*, Plato's protagonist Socrates posed the question, do the gods choose what is good because it is good, or is the good good because the gods choose it? If the first option is true, then the good is independent of the gods (or in a monotheistic faith, God). Good just is good and that is precisely why a good God will always choose it. But if the second option is true, then the very idea of what is good becomes arbitrary. If it is God's choosing something that makes it good, then what is there to stop God deciding that torture, for instance, is good? This is of course absurd, but the reason why it is absurd is that we believe that torture is wrong and *that is why* God would never choose it. To recognize this, however, is to recognize that we do not need God to determine what is right and wrong. Torture is not wrong *because* God chooses to say it is wrong, God says it is wrong because it *is* wrong.

The *Euthyphro* dilemma is a very powerful argument against the idea that God is required for morality. Indeed God cannot be the source of morality without morality becoming something arbitrary. There are attempts to wriggle off the prongs of the dilemma's forks, but like a trapped air bubble, pushing the problem down at one point only makes it resurface at another. For instance, some think the way out of the dilemma is to say that God just is good, so the question the dilemma poses is ill formed. If God and good are the same thing then we cannot ask whether God chooses good because it is good—the very question separates what must come together.

But the *Euthyphro* dilemma can be restated in another way to challenge this reply. We can ask, is God good because to be good just is to be whatever God is; or is God good because God has all the properties of goodness? If we choose the former answer we again find that goodness is arbitrary, since it would be whatever God happened to be, even if God were a sadist. So we must choose the second option: God is good because God has all the properties of goodness. But this means the properties of goodness can be specified independently of God and so the idea of goodness does not in any way depend upon the existence of God. Hence there is no reason why a denial of God's existence would necessarily entail a denial of the existence of goodness.

The *Euthyphro* dilemma is a convincing argument that right and wrong, goodness and badness do not depend on the existence of God. Without God anything is permitted only in the sense that there is no divine authority which will make sure you are punished for any wrongdoing or rewarded for being good. It's not surprising that we find this disturbing. The religious traditions of all the major monotheistic faiths have left us with a view of morality as a set of rules which we follow in order to be rewarded (eventually) and do not transgress in order to avoid punishment. No matter what is taught in Sunday schools about virtue's own rewards, the threats of punishment, more than promises of rewards, have been most psychologically effective in getting people to follow a religion's teachings. To believe that God is always watching you and will punish you for any wrongdoing is a very good way of keeping people in line.

However, removing belief in the divine enforcer is neither the end of morality nor the end of civilized behaviour. The joke about parking at the start of this chapter illustrates the point that human beings are able to make and enforce prohibitions for themselves. Everything will be permitted only if we choose to abandon ourselves to anarchy, and there is no reason why someone would want to do that just because they do not believe in God. Indeed, there is good evidence that levels of crimes are generally lower, and those of trust higher, in societies with low levels of religious belief.

It is an odd morality that thinks one can only behave ethically if one does so out of fear of punishment or promise of reward. The person who doesn't steal only because they fear they will be caught is not a moral person, merely a prudent one. The truly moral person is the one who has the opportunity to steal without being caught but still does not do so.

There is then a sense that the ethical atheist appears to have more moral merit than the religious believer who behaves ethically. Religion, with its threat of punishment and promise of reward, introduces a non-moral incentive to be moral that is absent in atheism, so the atheist's motives are less selfish. As it happens, I doubt that most religious people are good solely out of fear of God anyway. Most surely do not believe that it is only their fears of God and the law that stop them thieving, lying, and murdering. They should give others as much credit for basic decency as they do themselves.

Morality and choice

Another objection to the very possibility of a godless morality is the degree of personal choice it seems to leave to the individual.

If there is no single moral authority then do we all become sovereigns of our own privatized moralities? Many find this worrying. However, individual choice is an inescapable part of morality whether one believes in God or not.

I have already mentioned Kierkegaard's *Fear and Trembling* as a study of faith, but it is also a penetrating analysis of the inescapability of personal choice. This aspect of the work earned Kierkegaard his reputation as the 'father of existentialism'. Existentialist thinkers are a disparate bunch, comprising Christians, atheists, communists, fascists, free-spirits, and pretty much everything in between. What unites them is a belief in the inescapability and centrality of individual choice and freedom in human life. Their message is that we are always making choices and that these choices carry with them responsibility.

To avoid this heavy burden of responsibility we often try to pretend that we have not chosen. For instance, I might try to avoid making a choice by asking someone else to choose for me. Such was the case with a student who once came to Jean-Paul Sartre with a moral dilemma. His choice of the existentialist philosopher as his confidant indicated that he had in a sense already made up his mind about what to do. He knew Sartre would tell him, 'You are free, therefore choose.' He was seeking permission to make the choice for himself in order to diminish his responsibility for it. But to imagine he would thereby be absolved of responsibility is what Sartre called bad faith (*mauvaise foi*), a denial of one's own freedom. Even when we do not know what an adviser would say, if we select someone to defer to we are responsible for that choice. After all, I can always choose to accept or reject the advice given to me.

Kierkegaard's retelling of the story of Abraham illustrates this. Abraham is commanded by God to sacrifice his only son, Isaac (see Figure 6). On the divine command model of morality—that

6. Caravaggio, *Sacrifice of Isaac*, c.1603.

moral law comes directly from God—it seems that Abraham has no choice: he has to obey. But it would not be a great display of Abraham's faith and goodness if he just went ahead and killed his son without any thought at all. There are at least two choices he needs to make. The first is whether the command he has received is authentic. How can anyone know that they have received a genuine instruction from God rather than from an inner voice or an evil demon? No evidence or logic can settle this question conclusively. At the end of the day Abraham has to decide whether he is personally convinced or not. That is his decision.

The second choice is a moral one: does he follow the command? In a wonderful Woody Allen short story, Abraham thinks the answer to this is obvious: 'To question the Lord's word is one of the worst things a person can do.' However, when he goes ahead and takes his son to sacrifice, God is outraged that Abraham took his joke suggestion seriously. Abraham protests that at least his willingness to sacrifice his son showed he loved God. God replies that all it really proves is 'that some men will follow any order no matter how asinine as long as it comes from a resonant, well-modulated voice'.

The Allen story is a comic retelling of Kierkegaard's philosophical retelling of the Bible story and both make many of the same points. The most striking idea is that Abraham cannot evade his moral responsibility by simply following orders. We should be alert to this since the terrible human propensity to do awful things when they are commanded by someone in authority was particularly evident in the 20th century. Abraham's choice is not only to accept or reject God's authority. It is a moral choice to decide whether what he is being asked to do is right or wrong.

This relates to the independence of the ideas of God and the good established by the *Euthyphro* dilemma. As a matter of principle, it would not be right to do what God commanded (assuming you were satisfied that God really had commanded it) no matter what it was. If God asked you to lower someone innocent into acid inch by inch, killing them slowly in terrible pain, would that be okay? Of course it would not. Religious believers are sure that God would never ask such a thing (although the Old Testament God does ask for some pretty bloodthirsty deeds to be carried out). Whether he would or not, the point is that following or rejecting a command given to you by another, even God, is a matter of personal choice that carries moral responsibility.

The atheist and the believer are therefore in the same boat. Neither can avoid choosing which moral values to follow and taking responsibility for them. The atheist has the advantage, however, of being much more aware of this fact. It is easy for the religious believer to think that they can avoid choice just by listening to the advice of their holy men (it is usually men) and sacred texts. But since adopting this attitude can lead to suicide bombing, bigotry, and other moral wrongs, it should be obvious that it does not absolve one of moral responsibility. So although the idea of individuals making moral choices for themselves may sound unpalatable to those used to thinking about morality deriving from a single authority, none of us can avoid making such choices.

Sources of morality

So far I have argued that religion and morality, God and good, are separate. However, if we are to make a persuasive case that atheist morality is possible, it is not enough to show that religion cannot be the source of morality: we need to show what can be. Nor is it enough to show that we have to make moral choices for ourselves: we need to show that such choices carry moral weight.

However, it is not easy to identify the source(s) of morality. The difficulty can be seen by considering the strangeness of the question, 'Why should I be moral?' This question can have two kinds of answer. One is non-moral. For instance, one might say you ought to be moral because you will be happier if you are or God will punish you if you are not. These give us prudential reasons to be moral. The trouble is that sincerely believing in these reasons appears to undermine morality rather than support it. Acting morally because it is in one's own best interest to do so does not seem to be acting morally at all. Morality is about acting in the best interests of others and oneself.

However, if we give a moral answer to the question, such as 'be moral because that's what you ought to be', our justification is circular. Because the question is about why we ought to be moral at all, we cannot give a moral reason as part of the answer, since that would beg the question. We can only offer a moral reason for action if we are already persuaded of the merits of morality.

So we face a dilemma. If we want to know why we should be moral, our answer will either beg the question (if it offers a moral reason) or will undermine the morality of morality (if it offers a non-moral one). This is not just a problem for atheists. The same logic holds for everyone. The reasons to obey a god-given morality will either themselves be moral or non-moral and thus the same problem is faced by the religious believer.

The existence of this problem gives us strong reasons to doubt that we can find an objective source of morality, one that acts as its independent, perhaps transcendent foundation. However, it is not an argument against a morality which has more humble roots, within human nature. These roots are those of what Adam Smith called moral sympathy. In *The Theory of Moral Sentiments* (1759) he writes:

> How selfish soever man may be supposed, there are evidently some principles in his nature, which interest him in the fortunes of others, and render their happiness necessary to him, though he derives nothing from it, except the pleasure of seeing it. Of this kind is pity or compassion, the emotion we feel for the misery of others, when we either see it, or are made to conceive it in a very lively manner. That we often derive sorrow from the sorrows of others, is a matter of fact too obvious to require any instances to prove it; for this sentiment, like all the other original passions of human nature, is by no means confined to the virtuous or the humane, though they perhaps may feel it with the most exquisite sensibility. The greatest ruffian, the most hardened violator of the laws of society, is not altogether without it.

We have a natural concern for the welfare of others, a recognition that their welfare also counts. Total indifference to the welfare of others is not normal human behaviour, it is symptomatic of what we would normally call mental illness. This recognition of the value of others is not a logical basis of morality but a psychological one. This is part of what Hume was getting at when he said, 'reason is, and ought only to be the slave of the passions'. Moral reasoning can only get going if we have a basic altruistic impulse to begin with.

Where did this concern for others come from? It is sometimes naively believed that evolution cannot account for it, since natural selection is the survival of the fittest in which morality plays no role. The gene, after all, is selfish. But this objection commits the genetic fallacy: it confuses the explanation of morality's origins with its justification.

Evolutionary theorists actually have little difficulty explaining why moral impulses emerged. The survival of the fittest does not always mean the survival of the most physically strong or the most selfish. Humans do better when they cooperate. Being able to understand another's perspective and do things for them is essential for this. It's also much more efficient if such other-directed behaviour is motivated by emotions, which operate automatically, than by reasoning, which takes time and is error prone.

Once we have evolved the necessary requisites for benevolence, ethics can take on a life of its own and evolve as an artefact of human culture. It need not be a mere tool to help with our survival. Having been gifted by nature the capacity to see the value in others' lives and the ability to reason about what is in the best interest of all, morality is set free from its original survival function.

The answer to the question 'Why be moral?' is now clear enough. We should be moral because other people's (and arguably other animals') interests matter as much as ours do. This answer is only compelling if you can see and feel this for yourself. The psychopath cannot be reformed by rational argument. Those who insist that this is too flimsy a basis for morality are too pessimistic, since as a matter of fact it just is the basis of morality and despite too many aberrations, human beings have done a pretty good job of being mostly good to each other. To demand that morality must rest on something more objective and solid is to demand more than is necessary and more than can be provided.

I should briefly mention an alternative view, which is that we should just accept that the reasons to be moral are non-moral. Morality, on this view, is a kind of enlightened self-interest.

We haven't really risen above the tit-for-tat principle from which morality evolved. Believing this need not completely undermine morality. Giving money to charity, for example, is no less moral because it is done out of enlightened self-interest. What matters is that we act well. It need not matter that the ultimate justifications for so doing are selfish.

I am not persuaded by this because it does seem to me to be an indispensable part of morality that self-interest is not sovereign. Self-interest gives us reasons not to engage in anti-social behaviour or to do things that benefit us in the short run but have greater long-term costs. But that is not morality. Morality always contains the possibility of requiring one to act against one's own interests. If I am never prepared to sacrifice some self-interest, then I do not think I can ever be truly moral.

We can now return to the problems posed at the start of this section. First, if God isn't the source of morality, what is? I would argue along with evolutionary psychologists and philosophers such as Adam Smith and David Hume that it is a basic concern for the welfare of others, a concern that is not based on rational argument but empathy and, for want of a better phrase, our shared humanity.

The second problem was, if it is up to us to make our own moral choices, do these choices carry any moral weight? I would argue that they do. The seriousness of morality derives from the seriousness with which we take the interests of others and ourselves into account. Morality's importance is not diminished because moral decisions have to be freely chosen by us rather than dictated to us by laws laid down in heaven.

Moral thinking

Even if we accept that ultimate responsibility for our moral choices rests with us, we might still worry that we have no solid basis on which to make such choices. In the end, is morality simply a matter of personal opinion?

It would seem that way if you made the same false, sharp distinction between certain knowledge and mere opinion that gives rise to the idea that atheists should be agnostics. There is a continuum between the most objective facts which all competent judges would agree on and purely subjective preferences which are solely matters of personal taste. Judging skating or gymnastics competitions falls somewhere between the two ends of the spectrum. Although judges have to use their own judgement, there is still a high degree of objectivity which requires genuine expertise.

I'm sceptical that we could ever find a single moral theory that will provide us with a means of making moral judgements that always have as much objective validity as scientific findings. Still, I think that the wide agreement about such things as the goodness of honesty, generosity, and compassion, and the wrongness of wilful murder, rape, and theft, suggests we should not fear that morality is a morass of subjective opinion.

But why then do the major moral theories not agree? I suggest it is because each one lights upon one important dimension of moral thinking, but that none by itself gives us all the resources we need to live ethically. What we need to do to make good moral decisions is to consider what each theory draws our attention to and take all into account. In most general terms, these dimensions of moral thinking are character, consequences, duty, and care.

Take character first. Both Aristotle in ancient Greece and Confucius in ancient China taught that in order to live well one has to cultivate certain dispositions and character traits. They recognized that we are creatures of habit and that the best way of ensuring we act well is to practise doing well so that doing the right thing comes naturally. That does not mean that it always comes *automatically*, without thought. Because there are no hard-and-fast moral rules we need to practise what Aristotle called practical wisdom (*phronesis*) so we can make good judgements.

This approach has become known as *virtue ethics*. The virtues that Confucius and Aristotle believed make someone an exemplary person reflect their world and times, so we may not endorse every virtue they commended or praise some as highly. For instance, Confucius emphasized rank and social role, while Aristotle argued that the aristocratic virtue of 'magnificence' was one of the highest virtues. But most of what they praised remains praiseworthy today: modesty, honesty, trustworthiness, generosity, courage.

The idea that character matters more than moral principles rings true to experience. Think about the people you most admire for their ethics and you are sure to think of people who exude virtues such as kindness, compassion, or wisdom. They are not obsessed by what moral codes specify and when faced with a moral dilemma they do not set about solving it as though it were an intellectual puzzle.

A second dimension of moral thinking is to consider the consequences of our actions. To give a simple example, if I kick someone for no reason then that causes them pain. That pain is a bad thing which cannot in any way be outweighed by any better, good thing, because there is no reason for the kicking. Recognizing that the causing of this pain is a bad thing thus gives me a reason not to kick them. So we have reasons for not doing things that have bad consequences and we have reasons to do things that have good consequences, just because we recognize that it is better that good things happen than bad ones.

However, as soon as we try and build on this banal sounding truism to construct a complete *consequentialist* moral theory we head into difficulties. Most obviously, what if the action that has the best consequences overall requires us to cause harm to some innocent people? Should we sacrifice some innocent lives to save even more, other innocent lives? This was a very real question in the 2020 coronavirus pandemic. Was letting more people die to prevent society remaining in shutdown and to build herd immunity the right thing to do or a dreadful betrayal of the frail's basic right to life?

For reasons like these I'm not personally convinced that consequentialist thinking captures all that matters in moral reasoning. But it would be very strange to think it had no place at all. If our motivation is to do good, surely we have to think about whether the consequences of our actions are good or bad.

Consequentialist ethics tends to be radically impartial. You should consider the best consequences overall, not just for you or those close to you. The third dimension in moral thinking concerns our duties and so takes more account of the particularities of our relationships. For example, we have more responsibilities to look after our own children than we do children in general. In Confucian morality these relationships are so central that the philosopher Roger Ames calls it *role ethics*, meaning that every moral responsibility and obligation arises from and is situated in some kind of social relationship. Although some may be very broad, such as the duties you have as a citizen, none exists as a true universal, independent from our social position.

The *deontological* ethics of Immanuel Kant also concerns duties but in a more universal way. His 'categorical imperative' states, 'act only in accordance with that maxim through which you can at the same time will that it become a universal law'. This is similar to the 'golden rule' of Confucius: 'Do not impose on others what you do not wish for yourself.' Both are in essence pleas for *consistency*, or to put it another way, a demand to avoid hypocrisy. The principles that we use to judge our own actions should be no more lax than those we use to judge others. Moral rules are by their nature *universalizable*: what applies to one applies to all. The principle may sound technical, but it's simply a formalization of the colloquial maxim 'What's good for the goose is good for the gander'.

For Kant, universalizability is a necessary feature of a moral rule. Whenever we recognize that we ought to do something or ought not to do something else, we are endorsing a principle that is not relative to the particular interests, desires, or objectives of specific individuals, but universal and applicable to all. So, for example, to recognize that I ought not to be cheated is to recognize that no one ought to be cheated. To be indignant about being cheated while not worrying about cheating others is thus an example of hypocrisy: the arbitrary changing of rules to suit oneself.

A fourth factor in moral thinking is *care*. This is often thought to be a recent idea in Western philosophy, most associated with Carol Gilligan's ethics of care, developed in her 1982 book *In a Different Voice* (see Figure 7). Gilligan argues that the dominant modern theories in Western ethics are rule based and justified by rational arguments. This reflects the dominance of stereotypically male ways of thinking. This has occluded the importance of care, which is based more on sympathetic attention to people's individual needs rather than abstract general principles such as Kant's categorical imperative.

If we look back, however, we can see strands of this thinking in the ideas of moral sympathy developed by Adam Smith and David Hume, and also in the emphasis on relationships in Confucius. Gilligan turned the spotlight on this neglected side of moral philosophy, developing it further.

These families of approaches to ethics—based on character, consequences, duties, and care—demonstrate the richness of secular ethics. None require the positing of a divine rule-maker or

7. Carol Gilligan in 2011.

any other kind of transcendental source of morality. They show how the resources of good moral reasoning are available to the atheist and the religious believer equally.

Rather than view these as rival theories, I suggest we should see them all as resources we can draw upon to help in our moral reasoning. All capture something of importance, none captures everything. If we take such a pluralistic approach we will have to accept *Messy Morality*, as C. A. J. Coady bluntly puts in the title of his book. No one theory gives us a moral calculus that can be called into action to generate an appropriate response to any moral dilemma. Judgement is always needed, mistakes can always be made. Ethics is imperfect because it is part of the imperfect, infinitely variable human world, not a perfect other world.

Pulling up the roots?

Many remain unconvinced that secular ethics really can thrive without some kind of religious foundation. A popular argument, made increasingly in recent years by the likes of John Gray, Alister McGrath, and Nick Spencer, is that so-called secular ethics in the West is actually deeply rooted in religion. Pull up the Judaeo-Christian roots and your morality withers away.

The argument combines and arguably confuses two claims. The first is a historical one: that we only have the values we associate with the secular enlightenment and modernity because of the millennia of Christianity that preceded it. As Nick Spencer put it in his book *The Evolution of the West*, 'sometimes subtly, sometimes accidentally, sometimes egregiously, the role of Christianity in forming Western values that we hold dear is rewritten or forgotten'. The rights and dignity of the individual, for example, are rooted in the Christian idea of the sacredness of every single human life.

The second, stronger claim is that without a religious foundation, our ethics collapses like a house of cards. Spencer, for instance, argues that there is nothing to justify the liberal belief in the supreme value of the individual if we do not believe that everyone was created in the image of God. 'The foundational reason behind the Christian humanist commitment to human dignity is not available to atheists,' he argues, and none of the alternatives 'is quite up to the job'.

It should be clear that the first argument without the second is historically interesting but philosophically impotent. Even if it is true that the story of the development of Western values is inextricably linked with monotheism in general and Christianity in particular, it does not follow that those values cannot now stand on their own two feet. This is another example of the genetic fallacy: arguing for or against something on the basis of its origins rather than its actual nature. In any case, this story neglects the importance of Ancient Greek philosophy in Western moral thinking. This does not rest on monotheism, nor often on anything religious or transcendental at all.

So the only argument of any concern is the second: secular ethics cannot support itself without a transcendental platform. I have already outlined the case for why this is not so. Not only was there secular ethics in Ancient Greece, ethics has thrived outside of Christendom for millennia, including in China, where naturalistic understandings of the world have been dominant. Today, the most secular societies tend also to be the most moral, as measured by levels of trust, crime, homicide, equality, rights, and so on. Clearly ethics can and does exist without a religious basis. The insistence that it cannot does not fit the observed facts.

Why is the argument that ethics requires religion so popular? An important clue comes from a remark by John Gray, who wrote, 'Without a law-giver, what can a universal moral law mean? If you think of morality as part of the natural behaviour of the human animal, you find that humans do not live according to a single moral code.'

This gets to the heart of the misunderstanding. Gray is right that no secular ethics can claim the same absolute universalism and sovereignty of traditional God-given morality. If ethics is essentially human it will lack absolute authority and will admit of at least some variation in time and place. But that does not mean that we cannot have a secular ethics that is not real, powerful, and subject to a remarkable degree of agreement across cultures. The argument that godless ethics has no basis is only plausible if an impossibly high standard is set for how secure that basis must be.

It should now be obvious that the idea that the atheist must be an amoralist is groundless. The religious believer and the atheist share an important common ground. For both it cannot be that what is right and wrong, good or bad, is defined in terms of God or is simply dictated by divine command. Moral choices ultimately have to be made by individuals and we cannot get others to make them for us. So whether we have religious faith or not, we have to make our own judgements about what is right and wrong.

To provide a source for morality we need to do no more than sign up to the belief that certain things have a value and that the existence of this value provides us with reasons to behave in certain ways. This very broad commitment does not entail any specific philosophical or even religious position. It is arguably no more than the basic commitment of someone who has human feeling.

Once we have undertaken this basic commitment we have several resources to help us think about what the right thing to do is. We can think about what is required to help our own lives and those of others flourish. We can build our moral character and try to be more caring. We can think about the consequences of our actions and our particular duties. And we can strive to be consistent in our actions, or, to put it another way, to avoid hypocrisy.

Chapter 4
Meaning and purpose

What's the point?

'There's probably no God. Now stop worrying and enjoy your life.'

In 2008, a poster with this slogan appeared on London buses, supported by the scientist Richard Dawkins and the British Humanist Association (see Figure 8). The campaign was the brainchild of comedian Ariane Sherine, which goes some way to explain its light tone. However, it is in some ways *too* light. Despite the careful injection of some subtlety into the message by the inclusion of the word 'probably', the conclusion drawn is a little quick.

We can certainly stop worrying that without God society will descend into vice. But there is another worry that is not so easy to dismiss. If we are biological, mortal creatures who emerged through the random mutations of evolution, what is the point of living at all? If we have no purpose, where is life's meaning? Instead of the cheery bus poster, why not put instead the nihilistic mantra of the disenchanted and disappointed who see our existence as a vacuous tragicomedy: 'Life's a bitch and then you die'.

One assumption behind this fear of loss of meaning is that just as it is often assumed that ethics is yoked to religion and so without

8. Ariane Sherine and Richard Dawkins at the Atheist Bus Campaign launch.

religion ethics becomes impossible, so too are meaning, purpose, and religion packaged together as a set. To show why this is mistaken we have to go back to basics and consider what it means for any life to have a meaning or purpose.

The designer's purpose

If being given a purpose by a creator were enough to give meaning to something's existence, then meaning is found all around us. The French existentialist thinker Jean-Paul Sartre gave the example of a paper knife. This is designed with a clear purpose: to cut paper. In this way, it has what Sartre called an *essence*: an essential nature that is given by its intended purpose.

Sartre argued that without belief in God, humanity has no such essence. Human beings are not like paper knives, since an intelligent designer did not create us. However, it does not follow from this that life has no meaning, or even that it has no purpose. All that follows is that any such meaning or purpose is not a given, built-in to our essence. We are forced to create our own meaning, our own purposes.

Many have the intuition that any meaning which we ourselves give to life can only be a pale imitation of the kind of genuine meaning that would come from a creator. In fact, an argument can be made that it is the other way around. Purpose that is endowed is less meaningful than purpose that we choose or embrace. Go back to the knife. Although it is true that the knife has meaning and purpose because of its creator, this kind of purpose is hardly significant *for the knife*. When we ascribe a purpose to something in virtue of what it was made for, this locates the significance of that purpose with the creator or the user of the object, not in the object itself.

Knowing the purpose for which we were created does not necessarily make that purpose meaningful for us. Perhaps the opposite. Thomas Nagel asks us to imagine that 'we were being raised to provide food for other creatures fond of human flesh, who planned to turn us into cutlets before we got too stringy'. If asked for the meaning or purpose of our lives, we could say, 'to become food for human-munchers'. To think that answers the important existential question about the meaning of life would be absurd. Indeed we might judge that our lives were meaningless precisely because they had been reduced to the level of a mere instrument of others' will.

In short, a purpose or meaning given to a creature by its creator just isn't necessarily the kind of purpose or meaning that we are looking for in life when we wonder what the point of living is *for us*. If the only point in living is to serve *somebody else*'s purposes then we cease to be valuable beings in our own right and we merely become tools for others, like paper knives or cloned workers.

This is why a belief in a creator God does not automatically provide life with a meaning. It can only satisfy some people's desire for meaning under one of two conditions. The first is if the person decides that serving God is a good enough purpose in life for them. This seems odd to me, since I find it hard to imagine why God would want to create creatures like us solely to serve him. It's not as though he's in need of domestic help or anything like that. To be pleased to be such a servant seems unnervingly close in attitude to the people who for many centuries thought it was their role in life to work for the aristocracy and the upper classes. To take pride in one's lowly position and to see that as conferring meaning on one's life is indicative of what Nietzsche called 'slave morality': sanctifying what is in reality an unfortunate position so as to make that place seem much more desirable than it really is. This is self-deception: pretending to oneself that things are other than they really are in order to avoid uncomfortable truths.

A second way out for the religious is to trust that God has given us a purpose which is genuinely a purpose *for us* rather than merely something we do *for him*. We may not know what that is but we've got eternity to find out, so what's the rush? This is a perfectly coherent position, but as with much else in religion it has to be taken on blind trust, or, as the religious prefer to put it, on faith. To adopt this position is to admit that the religious actually don't have any clue what the meaning or purpose of life is, they simply trust God has a good one for them.

Purpose as goal

God or no God, if life is to be genuinely meaningful it must be so in a way which speaks to our own projects, needs, or desires and not just the purposes of whatever or whoever created us. This is why, incidentally, the theory of evolution doesn't provide life with any meaning either. Evolution tells us nothing about our purpose. It only explains how we have come to be at all. This no more explains the meaning of life than saying you were conceived because your parents wanted an heir. It gives part of the causal story of why you were born; it doesn't tell you why your life is significant, if indeed it is.

If we start thinking about life's meaning independently of the purposes of a creator, a natural way to start is by thinking about our own purposes or goals. People often talk about what they want to achieve with the implicit assumption that reaching these goals will fulfil them and make their lives meaningful.

In general, when people set themselves life goals they choose these goals themselves, and that is an important part of why those goals are meaningful for them. What people are doing is trying to achieve some form of 'self-actualization'. They set goals which they see as developing and fulfilling their potential so that they can become in a sense more than they now are. So, for example, someone with a talent for music might set goals which, if achieved, will show that they have developed their musical abilities to their fullest potential and hence that they have become a more complete or developed individual than they once were.

Sometimes athletes say things like 'God put me on earth to win the 200 m Olympic gold medal', but most of their peers will admit that winning is something they want and does God no favours at all. (It's also odd why God would create someone to win races and many more to lose them.)

However, there are some problems with locating life's meaning in one or more goals. The first is that there is always a risk that we do not achieve them. In areas such as athletics, it is inevitable that many more people fail to achieve their goals than succeed in doing so. But if a failure to hit the target is closely linked or is even a major part of what makes life meaningful then such a failure could be personally catastrophic. Setting easier targets avoids this risk at the cost of stripping the achievement of its value.

The second risk is that, having achieved our goals, life then becomes meaningless. This actually happens to some people who become very focused on one particular goal that takes many years to achieve. You will hear many a person say something like, 'I spent my whole life working towards achieving this and now that I've succeeded I don't know what to do with myself.' Often, since these people have very goal-directed personalities, the response is to set another goal and get back on the treadmill. This just highlights the problem of tying meaning too closely to goal achievement: life can never be truly satisfying except in those few moments around the achievement of each goal. At all other times, you are either working for the future goal or looking back on its past attainment.

What both problems have in common is that all meaning and value is tied to an achievement and everything else becomes a mere means to that end. In practice, however, the majority of us are not so narrowly goal-orientated or hungry for success. What most people want is companionship, a job they enjoy, and sufficient money for a good quality of life. Given all those things, life seems meaningful enough. You'd be missing something if you found yourself asking, 'Why would you want to do a job you enjoy all day and then go home to someone you love and fill your leisure time as you please?'

What you'd be missing is the insight that whether you have big goals or simply get on with life, the question of why you do anything at all has to stop somewhere with the simple answer 'because this is what I value'. Take the question of why we go shopping for groceries. For some it is an enjoyable leisure activity and that is reason enough. For most it is a means to an end, either to stay alive or to enjoy a nice meal. If you then ask 'but why enjoy a good meal or try to stay alive?' the only answer can be 'because I find meals and life worthwhile'. If we ask why we do *anything* in life, eventually we have to end up with things that are valuable in themselves and are not done simply to meet some further aim or goal. If we become too goal-fixated we risk missing this vital point.

That does not mean that the setting of goals cannot contribute to life's meaning. First, we often do find meaning in the process of striving towards those goals, not just in achieving them. Indeed, often the journey matters more than the destination. Many artists, for example, say that while working on a piece they are absorbed and imagine it will be their best yet, but when it is finished they are invariably disappointed. Being creative is what gives their lives meaning, and that is a process, not an outcome.

It's also true that sometimes achieving a goal leaves an enduring sense of satisfaction. Simply knowing one has set up a hospital, published a book, or raised a family can leave people feeling good rather than let down. In all such cases, there is a value to the means as well as to the ends. When we dedicate a lot of our lives to such valued action, if we have achieved our goals, we need not suddenly find our lives empty.

This suggests that although we commonly talk of the meaning or purpose of life, we should do better to think of its *value*. We need to know what makes life worth living, not what its end point is (which is death) or its deeper 'meaning' (it has none).

What makes life worth living? Any short answer will sound trite, but there really is no mystery about it. Ray Bradbury put it pithily in his short story, 'And the moon be still as bright'. This tells of Martians rather than humans, but the moral of the story translates:

> The Martians realized that they asked the question 'Why live at all?' at the height of some period of war or despair, when there was no answer. But once the civilization calmed, quieted, and wars ceased, the question became senseless in a new way. Life was now good and needed no argument.

When times are hard and things are going badly life can seem pointless. But when life is good there is no need to question. If one's work and home life are going well, it is in a way senseless to ask why such a life is worth living. The person living it just knows it is.

The specific ways in which life can have value are as numerous as the planet is populous. For some, tending to the garden is reason enough to get out of bed, for others it might be reading, helping others, being with friends, fighting for justice, baking, walking the dog. For almost all of us it is not just one thing but everything that we believe to be good in itself and not just something that serves as a link in a never-ending series of means to ends.

From this perspective, atheists could credibly claim that life is more meaningful for them than it is for many religious people who see this world as a kind of preparation for the next. When heaven is the ultimate destination, life on Earth isn't really valuable in itself. It is like a coin which can be exchanged for a good that really does count: the afterlife. This, however, merely postpones the question about what makes life worth living, since it doesn't tell us why life in heaven is meaningful in itself but life on earth isn't. Once again, religion does not so much provide an answer as ask us to accept on trust that an answer will be forthcoming.

Hedonism

It is often assumed that if this one life is all that we have, the only thing of real value in it is happiness or pleasure. 'Stop worrying and enjoy your life', as the bus poster commanded. Pleasure is certainly good in itself, and as long as it doesn't come at another's expense, it does not need any further purpose to justify it. In a material world, you might therefore conclude that the *only* real good is feeling good.

Arguably, this is the secular orthodoxy of our day. *Carpe diem*— seize the day—has become the motto for our times. Encouraged by the media, marketing, and advertising, we look for new and better pleasures all the time. If you were to spend just one day deliberately trying to spot how many newspaper and magazine articles and advertisements offer the promise of greater pleasure, you'd soon lose count. This is especially true if you read men's or women's lifestyle magazines, which seem to exist solely to offer the promise of a happier, more contented, sexually stunning you. If any of these tips actually worked, people would soon have no need to continue buying these magazines. Yet their circulations remain stubbornly high. I think that tells us something.

What is also revealing is that we are widely reported to be in general a rather dissatisfied society. In developed Western countries, we have access to more and better sources of pleasure than our predecessors could imagine. Yet we are not an especially fulfilled bunch. What's gone wrong?

This apparent paradox would not surprise most of the great philosophers of the past, almost all of whom have been suspicious of placing too great an emphasis on pleasure. The main problem, variously explained, is that pleasure is by its nature transitory. It is all very well feeling good, but pleasure does not in general leave a very long-lasting afterglow. Indeed, a life devoted to pleasure can be hard work, since if one is really serious about it, then one has to make a constant effort to get more and more. The fluid nature of time means that pleasures of the present are, from the moment they are attained, doomed to slip from our grip.

This is why a life devoted to pleasure is for most of us deeply unsatisfying. Moreover, shallow hedonism can in the long run lead to more pain than pleasure. The painter William Hogarth portrayed its perils in his series *A Rake's Progress* in which the debauched indulgence of a young heir leads to ruin, poverty, and syphilitic madness (see Figure 9).

Certainly a good life has its fair share of pleasure and only the most puritan of ethicists have claimed otherwise. But contentment or satisfaction requires more than just transitory pleasure. It requires us to be living the kind of lives that make us feel satisfied even when we are not particularly enjoying ourselves. There is no

9. It'll all end in tears: William Hogarth, *A Rake's Progress*—The Tavern Scene (1732–5).

formula for determining what kind of life this is, and it certainly varies considerably from person to person. For some, a hedonistic life does provide ongoing satisfaction as well as transitory pleasure. For others, a quiet, slow labour of love that to an outsider can seem quite joyless can be deeply rewarding.

The main point is simply that we should not be too quick to assume that if life's meaning is to be found in the living of the one life we have, then we should pursue a life of pleasure. That may fit the negative stereotype of the shallow atheist who seeks intoxication with pleasure to fill the emptiness of their purposeless lives, but it is as inaccurate a view of typical atheists as the joyless Bible basher is of the religious believer.

Curiously, although the religious can be quick to criticize the supposedly shallow hedonism of atheists, they tend to highly value happiness themselves. Whenever any study suggests that religious people are happier than non-believers, I have never yet heard a religious person say this is false or a terrible distortion of true faith. Rather, the fact that religion makes people happy is used as one of the major reasons to be religious. Even if they believe that the kind of deep happiness religion is supposed to bring surpasses the shallow variety available to atheists, happiness still remains the measure of value.

In any case, studies that claim that the religious are happier may not be making the right comparisons. If you look at the national level, the happiest societies tend to be the least religious. The most religious societies, in contrast, are those in which there is greatest insecurity, inequality, illness, and poverty.

So there is a paradox: religion appears to make people individually happier than their peers but collectively less happy than more secular societies. How can this be so? One reason is that if you drill down to the data, it is not religious belief that increases happiness but participation in a religious community. The happiness dividend appears to come more from a sense of belonging and support than religious conviction.

Another reason could be related to the explanation for why religious societies tend to be less happy in the first place. High levels of religious belief are most strongly correlated with insecurity. It is not difficult to see why: belief in divine providence can provide comfort and support when it is lacking in civil society. Similarly, within societies, those who believe God is taking care of them might be more shielded from the anxieties that life creates, even in the most advanced welfare states. This might be enough to make this group stand out in surveys.

Whether or not religious people are genuinely happier, it would be bizarre to make this a major debating point in the relative merits of atheism and religious belief. Happiness just isn't our only goal.

Most atheists value the truth and if religion is a comforting fiction, they would rather have less comfort than live with their eyes closed. Whatever such studies may say about the benefits of being religious, they say nothing about its truth.

Death

In traditionally religious societies, the onus is placed on atheists to explain how they can account for meaning, purpose, and value. But what happens if we turn the question on its head: why should anyone think that life *can't* have meaning or purpose for atheists?

The answer seems to be that the atheist, as a naturalist, unequivocally accepts human mortality, with no belief in afterlife, reincarnation, or dissolution of the ego as the self rejoins ultimate reality. But why should the fact of death make life any less meaningful? There can only be two explanations: one is that life needs to be *longer* than it actually is to be meaningful; the other is that life needs to be *endless* to be meaningful. Neither assumption survives scrutiny.

Take the idea that life can only have a meaning if it never ends. It is certainly not the case that only endless activities can be meaningful. Indeed, usually the contrary is true: some end or completion is often required for an activity to have any meaning. A football match, for example, gains its purpose only because it finishes after ninety minutes and there is a result. An endless football match would be as meaningless as a kick-around in the park. Plays, novels, films, and other forms of narrative also require some kind of completion. When we study we follow courses that end at a determinate point and don't go on forever. Innumerable human activities require some kind of closure or completion to make them meaningful.

We might even wonder whether life would be *less* meaningful if it never ended. What would be the point of doing anything if we had an eternity to live? Why bother trying to improve your golf swing or learn Finnish if you've always got time to do it later? Isn't it the knowledge of mortality, the sound of 'time's winged chariot hurrying near', that drives us and makes getting on with life meaningful at all?

It might be accepted that eternal life would indeed be meaningless if it were just more of the same of this life. But it would be meaningful if it were a different kind of life, perhaps an existence in some pure state of bliss or nirvana.

There are two problems with this. The first is that if eternal life is not at least similar to life on Earth then it is not clear how it could be lived by a person like you or me. Our whole *modus operandi* is one of embodied human beings with thoughts, feelings, plans, relationships, hungers, and disappointments. The life of a disembodied something, with no thought of past and future but just an eternal absorption in a feeling of bliss, seems to me to be nothing like my life at all. To be fair to the Indic traditions, this is what most teach. When the individual *atman* returns to the ultimate *Brahman*, the ego as we know it ceases to exist. Eternal life is an extinction of the self.

So we are faced with a dilemma. Either the afterlife is recognizably like this life, in which case an eternal one does not look very meaningful; or it is not like this life at all, in which case it doesn't look like the kind of life we could actually live.

The second problem with the idea that eternal life is a special state is that it assumes that some states are worth being in for their own sake. The whole point about nirvana is that we do not need to ask what the point of being in that state is—it is simply valuable in itself. But if we accept that some forms of existence can be worth living for themselves, then why ignore the valuable form of life we actually have and instead hold out some hope for an idealized form of life to come?

So the idea that life needs to be eternal to be meaningful is simply false. What of the alternative suggestion that it needs to be much longer to be meaningful? Human life is, by the measure of the universe, a blink of an eye. This is very unpersuasive. If finite life can have meaning then it seems odd to think that it must have a certain length. It is true that life can fly by distressingly quickly. Yet at the same time, for every person who reaches old age still hungry for life, there is another who has been worn out by life's ups and downs and is getting tired. Life may not be the perfect length, but it is long enough to be meaningful.

Some think that it is the perfect length, not because nature has made us lucky, but because we live our lives according to what is the norm. If the average lifespan were longer we wouldn't lead more meaningful lives, we would just adjust our life plans accordingly by, for instance, being in less of a hurry to establish ourselves in careers.

This is a comforting thought, but I find it hard to believe that life could not be improved by several extra decades, provided they could be lived in good health. There is so much life has to offer that three score years and ten does seem a rather mean allotment. Accepting one's mortality is not the same as believing that this is the best of all possible worlds. Not only is our average lifespan on the short side, too many people do not even live that long.

We're left with the somewhat paradoxical position that mortality is required to make life meaningful, but death is almost certain to come too soon. That's why I think it is possible to overstate the typical atheist's acceptance of our mortality. Atheists no more want to die than anyone else. Indeed, Aristotle argued that the more a person is living a flourishing life, 'the more he will be pained at the thought of death; for life is best worth living for such a man, and he is knowingly losing the greatest goods'.

If death is a sadness even for those who have had a good innings, it is even grimmer for those whose lives have been deeply troubled, unhappy, or unfulfilling. It is perhaps the absence of any hope of salvation or redemption for such people that makes the fact of death so hard to accept. It should, however, be noted that in most religions that preach an afterlife, salvation is not for all anyway, and that, worse, unbelievers face an eternity in hell, along with grievous sinners. That aside, it is an inevitable feature of atheism's realistic naturalism that the universe, which cares for nothing at all, cannot be expected to operate in the ways we would like.

Death thus occupies a crucial role in the atheist worldview. If we pretend or imagine that life's purpose lies outside life itself, we will be searching the stars for what is underneath our feet all the time. It is the final full stop that makes life meaningful. The curtain falling on *Othello* does not ruin the play, it's a necessary condition for it being any good in the first place. But that does not mean that when death comes it is not a cause for regret or sadness, especially when it comes too soon. We may regret death while at the same time knowing that its inevitability is what makes life so valuable. Life can be worth living in itself, even in difficult times, and there is no need for it to serve any other purpose.

Meaningful lives

Although I have here argued the case for the possibility of meaningful atheist lives, perhaps it is more persuasive simply to point to the reality of such lives. Many atheists do and have lived meaningful and purposeful lives and for others to deny this seems to be remarkably arrogant.

One such atheist is Arundhati Roy, award-winning author of *The God of Small Things* and a campaigner for social change and justice in India. In an interview, asked if she thought death was the end, she replied, 'Yes . . . sometimes even before you die, that's it.' I think this sharp reply shows how an atheist belief in mortality can motivate a real concern for those who, though still living, are not getting a good chance to enjoy the only life they have.

Interestingly, a lot of famous atheists are writers, thinkers, or artists. Milan Kundera, Czech author of *The Unbearable Lightness of Being*, is an atheist, while the late Terry Pratchett, author of the *Discworld* novels, said, 'I think I'm probably an atheist, but rather angry with God for not existing.'

Perhaps the biggest challenge to people who think atheists cannot live meaningful lives are countries such as France, the Czech Republic, and Sweden, where between 34 and 40 per cent of the population doesn't believe in 'any sort of spirit, god or life-force'. Take a holiday to Paris, Prague, or Stockholm and see if you're overcome by a wave of meaninglessness.

History is also populated with a good number of atheists, including the former French president François Mitterrand (1916–96), American physicist Richard Feynman (1918–88), the science fiction writer Isaac Asimov (1920–92), and Nobel prize winning chemist and physicist Marie Curie (1867–1934). Many others, such as Andrew Carnegie and Benjamin Disraeli, were not religious and might have been confirmed atheists in more tolerant times.

I am not saying that all of these people are heroes or that we should admire all they did. Atheists live good and bad lives, just as priests, popes, and rabbis do. The point is simply that these are all lives lived with purpose, values, and meaning, concrete proof that a life without belief in God is not a life without direction or significance. The greatest proof that something is possible is to show that it actually exists. These people show that meaningful atheist lives are more than theoretical possibilities. They are around us every day.

The kind of atheism that celebrates the one life we have and our ability to live it ethically is often called secular humanism. Secular humanism is simply an atheism that affirms the possibility of living purposeful and moral lives. Today, the qualifier 'secular' is often considered redundant, but because there are traditions of religious humanism it remains the most accurate label.

However, many, perhaps most atheists who fit this description do not self-describe as humanists. One reason is that most countries have organized humanist membership associations, and so the humanist identity is often tied to those groups rather than to a worldview. 'Humanism' is also an ambiguous term, with a tradition of Christian humanism, for example.

Another reason why people might not identify as humanist is that the very name may have become associated with the hubristic idea of the superiority of the human race and the desire to celebrate and further the good of the species. Many atheists and other types of humanist reject this because they do not see any reason to glorify *Homo sapiens* or make the species our sole focus. Rather, our concern should be with individual lives, and also perhaps the welfare of other sentient species.

For me, the terms positive atheist and secular humanist are coterminous. The question of how we self-identify is not critical. After all, many studies suggest that most atheists do not describe themselves as atheists, perhaps because they falsely believe that atheism is dogmatic or nihilistic.

Don't honk if you're an atheist

Most atheists see themselves as steely realists. Their atheism is a part of their willingness to square up to the world as it is and face it without recourse to superstition or comforting fictions. Such realism requires us to accept that much of what goes on in this world is unpleasant. Bad things happen, people have miserable lives, and you never know when blind luck (not purposeful fate) might intervene to change your own life, for the better or for the worse.

Because of this, atheists tend to find relentless, blind cheeriness anathema. They both smile and wince at evangelical Christians with their bumper stickers asking you to 'honk if you love Jesus'. Happy-clappy atheism is just as objectionable and there is a tendency for atheists to overstate how great life can be without God. Several secular humanist organizations around the world have even adopted the 'happy humanist' icon as their logo.

Fortunately, atheism's inherent realism provides, on the whole, a kind of immunity to excess. The truth is that there is no necessary link between being an atheist and having a positive or negative outlook. In arguing that atheism can be positive, I am not claiming that becoming an atheist is a passport to happiness. Fulfilment in this life is harder work than that and it is a mark of atheism's realism and optimism that an acceptance of this sober truth still leaves fulfilment within our reach.

No atheism that is rooted in a reasoned naturalism can ever be all sunshine and roses. There are also shadows and thorns. One typical way of thinking about atheism shows why this must be so. Many atheists throughout history have compared their belief with a form of growing up. Freud, for instance, saw religious belief as a kind of regression to childhood. With religion, we are like children who still believe that we are protected in the world by benevolent parents who will look after us. It is no coincidence that God is referred to as father in the Judaeo-Christian tradition.

Atheism requires accepting that we have to make our own way in the world without any unquestionably good, divine guardians to always protect us. This realism means atheism cannot ever be presented as an undiluted, positive joy. Real life is about accepting ups and downs, the good and the bad, the possibility of failure as well as the ambition to succeed. Atheism is a sincere attempt to confront the truth about our human condition without the shield and comfort of religion or superstition.

The right attitude to life and death seems to me to be captured in Japanese philosophy and culture, where there is a sensitivity to imperfection and impermanence called *mono no aware*. It is most evident during *Hanami*, the festivities that occur during the cherry blossom season. People picnic under the blooms, delighting in their beauty but acutely aware for how briefly they flower before being blown away. The bitter and the sweet coexist, intensifying each other, making us delight in being alive and sad at the prospect of death.

Chapter 5
Atheism in history

Who were the first recorded atheists? The question is harder to answer than you might think. When we read about ancient belief systems, it is difficult to understand them as they really were, rather than through the lens of our contemporary concepts and categories. Terms like 'naturalism', 'supernatural', and 'atheism' would have made little sense to many people in history.

For the most part, humans appear to be instinctively *animists*, seeing the whole of nature as being alive. This can be understood in purely naturalistic terms. As well as the kind of naturalism in the contemporary West which sees the universe as a kind of inert mechanism there is another kind which sees nature as a single organism. However, in almost all societies it seems that the animist impulse has given rise to belief in spirits or gods of some kind.

Still, this impulse has not been universal, or at least it has not always been acted on. For example, we can be fairly confident that there were atheists in BCE India. Most obviously, the Cārvāka (or Lokāyata) school was robustly materialist and so had no place at all for supernatural entities.

The picture in China is less clear. China has the largest proportion of convinced atheists of any country in the world: 61 per cent according to one major survey. This surely has a lot to do with decades of communism. But before Mao came to power, Chinese thought had been very naturalistic for millennia. The dominant Confucian tradition has mostly confined itself to the immanent world of the here and now. 'All who speak about the natures of things, have in fact only their phenomena to reason from, and the value of a phenomenon is its being natural,' as the 4th-century BCE Confucian Mengzi wrote. This long history of naturalistic thought might in part explain why.

The claim that Chinese thought is naturalistic might seem perverse given the emphasis on *yin* and *yang*, ancestor worship, and the way of heaven. But properly understood these have all been seen as part of the natural world. *Yin* and *yang*, for instance, are not supernatural forces but principles which govern nature. They are most important in Daoism, a philosophy which venerates the natural world.

Even rituals which appear to be supernatural seem to be more about providing structure to life and society than pleasing spirits. The 3rd-century BCE Confucian Xunzi, for example, asked why it is that people perform rain sacrifices when sometimes it then rains and sometimes it doesn't. 'One performs divination and only then decides on important affairs. But this is not for the sake of getting what one seeks, but rather to give things proper form.'

It is also important to note that both Confucianism and Daoism are philosophies, not religions in any conventional sense. Just as Western philosophy was born in Miletus when Thales et al. ditched myth for reason, so Chinese philosophy emerged in Qufu when Confucius presented his reasoned teachings. Having dismissed them for centuries, Western philosophers increasingly accept that they are rational systems of thought.

In the West, there are two answers to the question of when atheism was born which may appear to be in conflict with one another. One is that atheism began at the dawn of Western civilization itself, in Ancient Greece. The other is that atheism only appeared as late as the 18th century. The conflict is, however, merely apparent, for there is a single story which is consistent with both accounts. This is that atheism has its origins in Ancient Greece and although there have always been people who did not believe in God, atheism did not emerge as an overt and avowed belief system until late in the Enlightenment.

The historian of religion James Thrower makes the case for a birth in Ancient Greece on the basis that atheism is in essence naturalism. Naturalism in the West starts with the pre-Socratic Milesian philosophers of the 6th century BCE: Thales, Anaximander, and Anaximenes. Whereas previously the origins and functions of the world were all explained by gods and myths, the Milesians worked on the then revolutionary idea that nature could be understood as a self-contained system operating according to laws that are comprehensible by human reason. This marked a fundamental shift in the orientation of explanatory accounts. No longer was it necessary to postulate anything outside of nature to understand how nature worked: the answers were all to be found within nature itself.

This therefore also marked the point where science began, although it would be a long time before it matured into what we would now recognize as rigorous experimental science. However, science is only one of the fruits of the new rational way of looking at the world initiated by the pre-Socratics. Consider the development of history in Ancient Greece between the works of Herodotus and Thucydides, as discussed by Thrower and the philosopher Bernard Williams in his *Truth and Truthfulness*. An important boundary was crossed (albeit not in one clean leap) when Thucydides set out to discuss history as a series of factual and dated events which fit together to tell some kind of causal story. As Williams puts it, the histories of Thucydides aimed at 'telling the truth' as it is. Previously, it had been about recycling myth and hearsay, often with a political or moral purpose. The view of history offered by Thucydides is now so commonsensical (though not to many academic historians) that it is difficult to imagine how people could ever have thought of history otherwise. This only underlines how radical a development Thucydides' history was.

The connection between the development of Milesian philosophy and Thucydidean history is not just their common rejection of myth but what both brought in to replace it: rationality. A rational account is broadly one which confines itself to reasons, evidence, and arguments that are open to scrutiny, assessment, acceptance, or rejection on the basis of principles and facts which are available to all. An optimally rational account is one where we don't have to plug any gaps with speculation, opinion, or any other ungrounded beliefs.

The science for which the pre-Socratics laid the foundations and the approach to the study of history begun by Thucydides are both characterized by their rational nature. History becomes the attempt to tell the story of the past based on evidence and arguments which are available to and assessable by all. Science becomes the attempt to give an account of the workings of the world based on evidence and arguments which are available to and assessable by all.

The naturalism which lies at the heart and root of Western atheism is therefore itself rooted in a broader commitment to rationalism. (This kind of rationalism-with-a-small-r is not to be confused with the 17th-century Rationalism-with-a-capital-R, which is much more specific and ambitious in the claims it makes for the power of rationality.) Naturalism is the worldview that emerges when you follow the method of rationalism and so it is rationalism, rather than naturalism, which is most fundamental to the origins of atheism. That is another reason why atheism does not entail a shallow commitment to the primacy of scientific enquiry but to the value of rational explanation, of which science is merely one spectacularly successful example.

Despite the distinctively atheistic hue of plenty of Ancient Greek thought, the historian David Berman is struck by how late atheism emerged as an explicitly held belief system in the West. Thrower, in accord with Berman, says that Baron d'Holbach, whose *The System of Nature* was published in 1770, was the 'first unequivocally professed atheist in the Western Tradition'. Berman claims the first such work to be published in Britain was the *Answer to Dr Priestley's letters to a philosophical unbeliever* in 1782. The authorship of this work is disputed, and it is possible that it is the work of two men, William Hammon and Matthew Turner.

Before the late 18th century we had isolated works that could be viewed as atheist, such as some writings of Democritus and Lucretius. There were even periods in history when the God or gods were seen as irrelevant in at least some sectors of society, such as in the upper classes of the early Roman Empire. But there was no systematic and ongoing attempt to present and promulgate a godless worldview as an alternative to the religious one.

Although it has become fashionable to debunk the ideals of the Enlightenment, its most basic ideals are now considered fundamental. We may debate the precise meaning of equality, liberty, and tolerance, but all three are central to our notion of what makes a good and fair society. We may have lost some of the more enthusiastic Enlightenment thinkers' optimism in the power of reason, but we would certainly not like to go back to a society based on superstition. And although some may think that we have gone too far in our disrespect of authority, few seriously believe that we should return to a time when office was inherited, when only the male upper and middle classes were politically enfranchised, or when leading clerics wielded strong political power. Despite its faults, the Enlightenment has to be seen by any reasonable person as an important stage in the progression of Western society.

It would be too strong to say that because avowed atheism emerged riding on the back of the Enlightenment it should take the credit for its achievements. But it would be equally foolish to see the simultaneous emergence of modern atheism and the Enlightenment as purely coincidental. Their arrival at the same point in history is at least suggestive of a connection, and it is not hard to see what that is. Atheism takes the Enlightenment rejection of superstition, hierarchy, and rationally ungrounded authority to what many would see as its logical conclusion.

However, the failure of the Enlightenment to usher in a new era of popular atheism reflects how deeply religion is embedded in Western culture. One of the most fascinating features of Berman's history is how writers in the 17th century often denied even the possibility that anyone could ever be a genuine atheist—someone who really believed there was no God as opposed to someone who just acted as if there were none. Religion was assumed to be universal. Denying the existence of God was as inconceivable as denying the existence of the sun or stars.

Indeed, some used the supposed universal belief in God as an argument for God's existence. This variation on the old adage, 'Fifty million Frenchmen can't be wrong' is rather weak for a rational argument. Widespread agreement cannot make something true or false. After all, at one time nearly the whole world's population thought that rain came from the gods or that the earth was the centre of the universe. The only thing widespread belief in religion shows is that atheism has been battling against the odds. No wonder it finds it so hard to shake off its image as a purely negative denial of the religious norm.

Yet in a little over 200 years atheism has won over millions of adherents—especially, it has to be said, intelligent or educated people. It has established itself as a credible alternative to religion, contrary to almost unanimous opposition. This is also a reminder of how little experience we have of living our lives and ordering our societies without the backdrop of religion. Mass atheism is young and as such we must expect to see some signs of its immaturity.

Reason and progress

The story of atheism's development in the West is routinely told in terms of the rise of reason and the march of progress. Many atheists would say that once we were prepared to look at religion with the cool eye of reason, its untruth became self-evident. It is obviously not the product of divine revelation but of particular, local human practices. On this view, it is impossible to take Enlightenment ideals seriously and cling on to the belief that religion opens the door to truth. The emergence of avowed atheism in the late Enlightenment can therefore be placed in a story of the ongoing progress of human society and intellect, even though that progress is uneven and reversible.

However, this story becomes less convincing when you recognize that the history of Western atheism is not the history of global atheism. In India, there has been no significant progress from more religious to more naturalistic worldviews. If anything, the influence of Cārvāka has waned over the centuries, not grown. If both early Buddhism and late Zen appear to be very naturalistic, many of Buddhism's iterations have more, not fewer, supernatural elements. It is therefore far too simplistic to see atheism as part of a wider, progressive story about the development of human intellect and understanding.

It is sometimes also objected that atheists are too in thrall to reason anyway. 'There are more things in heaven and Earth than are dreamt of in your philosophy,' as Shakespeare's Hamlet said. But intelligent atheists have never had any problem with accepting there is more in the world than we can currently rationally explain, and some things may forever be beyond us. For example, many would agree that we do not have a rational explanation for how consciousness can be produced in physical brains, but there are rational reasons to suppose consciousness exists. It can be rational to believe in the existence of what cannot yet be rationally explained.

That is not the same as believing in things we have no rational reason to think even exist. In the case of, say, ghosts, we not only lack a rational explanation of how ghosts can exist, we also lack any rational reasons to suppose that they do. If you thought that we should believe in things we have no rational reason to think exist, why not believe in the tooth-fairy? Non-atheists may get irritated when entities such as the tooth-fairy and Santa Claus are invoked to illustrate the ridiculousness of permitting belief in what is not rational, but such irritation does not comprise a serious counter-argument.

If you believe we have good reasons for believing in God but not in the tooth-fairy then the criticism of atheists should not be that they are too enamoured of reason but that they are not reasoning well enough.

The 20th century and beyond

Despite the growth of atheism, suspicion, and even fear, of atheists remains widespread. As recently as 2019, 31 per cent of Americans told pollsters they would not vote for a presidential candidate from their own party that they judged to be 'generally well-qualified' if the candidate were an atheist.

It's not difficult to find religious leaders and thinkers who dread the trend towards a more secular society. Britain's former chief rabbi, the late Jonathan Sacks, called a 'godless society' a 'real danger', blaming it for 'four terrifying experiments in history, the

French Revolution, Nazi Germany, the Soviet Union and communist China'.

The real story of atheism's role in modern horrors is much more complicated. For instance, the place of religion in fascism varied enormously and is sometimes difficult to interpret. In Spain, the Catholic Church was on the side of the fascist Franco in the civil war and continued to support him for many years after he came to power, with serious dissent of any kind not emerging until the 1960s. Indeed, many saw the civil war as a kind of religious crusade against the godless Republicans. There is still a great deal of controversy concerning the extent to which members of the Catholic prelature Opus Dei occupied positions of power in Franco's Spain. This was not an atheist fascism but an expressly Catholic one.

In Italy too, the Vatican signed the notorious Lateran Treaty with the fascist government in 1929, providing mutual recognition of fascist Italy and the Vatican state. Under Mussolini Roman Catholicism became the official religion of Italy. At no time was there a clear majority in the Catholic Church opposed to his regime, even after 1938 when anti-Jewish laws were passed.

The case of Nazi Germany is the most important one, for it was under Hitler that the worst fascist atrocities took place. But Nazi Germany was not a straightforwardly atheist state. Hitler's own religious beliefs are not fully known and are keenly contested, but publicly at least he maintained the traditional German view of women as needing to focus on 'Kirche, Kuche, Kinder'—Church, kitchen, and children.

More concretely, a concordat was signed between the Nazi government and the Catholic Church in 1933. The collusion between the Protestant Churches and the Nazi regime was even closer, helped by an anti-Semitic tradition in German Protestantism. Resistance came not from the established

Protestant Churches but by the breakaway Confessional Church, led by pastors Martin Niemöller and Dietrich Bonhoeffer. These dissidents are rightly held up by Christians today as shining examples of principled resistance to Nazism, but the fact that they had to leave the established Church to lead this resistance is no cause for Christian celebration.

Indeed, historian Kristen Renwick Monroe has argued that 'Religion played an integral part in the Holocaust. Christian churches from the time of Constantine in the fourth century had wanted to convert Jews, and medieval Christian churches throughout Europe engaged in varying degrees of persecution because they felt it was the Jews who had crucified Christ.' Anti-Semitism was an integral feature of Christianity and, says Renwick Monroe, 'was never contradicted, or even addressed directly, by any religious group throughout this period'.

Things are rather different when it comes to communism. In China, the accusation that the atheism of Maoism is in part responsible for its awfulness is somewhat blunted by the realization that China had long been a Confucian rather than a religious society anyway. One godless system was replaced by another.

The Soviet Union was an avowedly and officially atheist state which saw, under Stalin's rule in particular, mass extermination on a horrific scale. But this is no more reason to think that atheism is necessarily evil than the fact that Hitler was a vegetarian is a reason to suppose that all vegetarians are Nazis. It is certainly a historical refutation of the idea that atheism must always be benign. But it is a very naive atheism that maintains it is impossible for atheists ever to do wrong. Christian critics who think that the Soviet Union provides some kind of refutation of atheism would, by their own logic, have to accept that atrocities such as the crusades or inquisitions refute Christianity. Stalin's terror was not an inevitable or logical consequence of atheist beliefs. The mere existence of millions of humane atheists in Western democracies who have no truck with state communism shows that there is no essential link between being an atheist and condoning the gulags.

In fact, even though the Soviet Union was officially atheist, it is not even true that it always had an antagonistic relationship with the Church. Stalin (see Figure 10) permitted the formation of the Moscow Patriarchate, a central body for the Russian Orthodox Church. According to historian Michael Bordeaux, throughout the years of Soviet rule the Patriarchate 'overtly backed every military initiative of the Soviet regime: suppression of the Hungarian uprising (1956), the erection of the Berlin Wall (1961), the invasion of Czechoslovakia (1968) and Afghanistan (1979)'.

10. Joseph Stalin in 1942: not the best advert for atheism.

Post-Soviet claims that the Church had opposed the Soviet regime all along just don't wash.

Those who fear an atheist state should be reassured that most atheists don't want one either. Since the Enlightenment almost all atheists have advocated state secularism, in which the state is neutral on matters of personal belief that do not interfere with the rights of others to hold theirs. State secularism has been one of the great triumphs of Western civilization and one of the proudest legacies of the Enlightenment. Many religious believers support it because it guarantees religious freedom in a way in which a state with an official religion cannot.

Secular democracies have been the most successful societies in history, measured by health, wealth, liberty, and all other elements of human flourishing. When asked whether religion was important in their daily life, three-quarters or more of people polled in Estonia, Sweden, Denmark, Norway, the Czech Republic, and Japan said no. These are countries that all score very highly in other league tables of human flourishing such the UN's annual world happiness league tables, equality indices, rankings of health outcomes and crime rates, and so on. People are quick to lay the blame for recent history's atrocities at atheism's door but any objective study will confirm that one of the greatest predictors of how well a country is doing is how many of its citizens have no religion.

There are, I think, several interesting insights into atheism which can be gleaned by looking at its history. The first is that the rise of atheism is essentially linked to the growth of rational thought as the primary means of understanding the world. Atheism is thus part of a progressive story of human culture in which superstition is replaced with rational explanation and where we lose the illusions of the supernatural realm and come to learn how to live within the natural one.

The second is that atheism is not to be blamed for the terrors of 20th-century totalitarianism. On the contrary, atheists have been among the most fervent advocates of a neutral, secular state in which all have the freedom to believe or not. What's more, in societies where people use that freedom to give up their religion, the result tends not to be amoral anarchy but greater peace, prosperity, and happiness.

Chapter 6
Atheism in the 21st century

The New Atheism

At the dawn of the 21st century, the position of atheism was fairly stable around the world. In much of East Asia it remained a long-standing feature of the belief landscape, across the West it was a slowly growing but minority position, while almost everywhere else it remained largely unknown and often unspeakable.

Early in this century, however, Western atheism suddenly came to much greater prominence. In 2006 the journalist Gary Wolf labelled the new, assertive movement that was emerging 'the New Atheism', a name that stuck. A number of New Atheist books became surprise bestsellers. First, from the USA came Sam Harris's *The End of Faith* (2004) then from the UK Richard Dawkins's *The God Delusion* (2004). Daniel Dennett's *Breaking the Spell* (2006) and Christopher Hitchens's *God Is Not Great* (2007) completed a transatlantic quartet. When all of these writers met for a recorded discussion, the resulting video was known as 'The Four Horsemen', an ironic allusion to the biblical apocalypse.

Although the most prominent New Atheists were all anglophone, the New Atheism created waves across the West, with *The God*

Delusion translated into thirty-five languages. Michel Onfray's 2005 *Traité d'athéologie* (An Atheist Manifesto, also published in English as *In Defence of Atheism: The Case Against Christianity, Judaism, and Islam*) brought some of the New Atheist fire to France and elsewhere in translation.

New Atheism was a singular term applied to a diverse number of people. Dennett in particular is an outlier, less confrontational and more philosophically nuanced than his peers. Still, the rest of the main players had enough in common for the grouping to make sense. The New Atheists were, for the most part, strongly critical of both moderate and fundamentalist religion, dismissive of the idea that they should avoid offending the faithful, and convinced that religious belief was profoundly irrational. Their self-confidence and forcefulness came as a shock in societies where criticism of religion had generally been mild and atheists had been at the margins.

New Atheism was yet to come when the first edition of this book was published in 2003. I did, however, devote a section of the book to what I called 'militant atheism'. This is any form of atheism which is actively hostile to religion in almost all its forms. To be hostile in this sense requires more than just strong disagreement—it requires something verging on hatred and is characterized by a desire to wipe out all forms of religious belief. Less militant atheists may believe just as strongly in the falsity of religion, but although they would perhaps think that in an ideal world it would not exist, they are generally relaxed about the persistence of moderate religious beliefs, believing that faith can sometimes inspire goodness in people.

The New Atheists seemed to fit the description of militants, but most resent the charge. They are most indignant about being called 'fundamentalists' as though they were the mirror image of the religious variety. As Dawkins rightly protests, 'I am not going to bomb anybody, behead them, stone them, burn them at the stake, crucify them, or fly planes into their skyscrapers'.

Another strong response is that a degree of militancy is required since there are still too many parts of the world where atheists are persecuted and even killed. Atheism is punishable by death in more than a dozen nations, including Iran, Malaysia, Nigeria, Pakistan, Qatar, Saudi Arabia, and the United Arab Emirates. In *The God Delusion* Dawkins rightly wrote, 'the status of atheists in America today is on a par with that of homosexuals fifty years ago'. In 2004 there were openly gay mayors and members of congress and the senate, but no openly atheist ones. Surveys have repeatedly shown that Americans would be less happy for their children to marry an atheist than a member of another faith. There was arguably a need to be vocal and assertive and it is indeed true that since the charge of the Four Horsemen, atheism has been growing in popularity and acceptance in the USA.

The distinction between 'moderate' and 'militant' atheists remains problematic, not least because some see them as loaded terms. More fundamentally, they represent ends of a spectrum rather than two discrete camps. The New Atheists lie closer towards the militant end. But because they came to such prominence many towards the other end have been concerned that the New Atheism has created a misleading impression of what mainstream atheism stands for.

The New Atheism has thus undermined the claim that atheism is not in essence a negative position and that atheists are not all obsessed by attacking religion. The New Atheists made their strong opposition to religion central, saying much less about the positive aspects of naturalism. The very titles of their books emphasized this even more. All were about the horrors of religion, none about the benefits of atheism.

More moderate atheists could be justly aggrieved by this. This objection to the New Atheism is more about tactics and rhetoric than substance. That does not, however, make it any less legitimate. When we speak and write we need to think not only about the cogency of our arguments but the effects our words are going to have on others. Even if every single negative claim were true, it would still be the case that collectively they helped create an image of atheism in the public imagination as pugilistic, anti-religious, and uncompromising. While some may welcome this, many see it as unfortunate.

Atheists are *necessarily* anti-religious in one sense only: they believe that religions are false. But in this sense of the word 'anti' most Muslims are anti-Christian, most Christians anti-Jewish, most Protestants anti-Roman Catholic, and so on. This is not necessarily or usually an anti of antagonism. Atheists are no more required to be hostile to the religious than Jews are required to be hostile to Hindus. Atheist opposition to religion always entails an opposition to its truth, but not always to its alleged perniciousness or to its followers.

There are, however, also substantial disagreements between the New Atheists and many of their equally godless critics. These concern whether religion is not just false but demonstrably and absurdly so, and whether it is always harmful.

God delusions

There is an intellectual self-confidence and assertiveness about the New Atheists. It is not just that they believe religion is false, but that anyone who used their brain would see that it was. New Atheists take the view that religious belief is almost always obviously unreasonable and that therefore it is dishonest and unnecessary to pretend there is room for reasonable disagreement. It can be conceded that some religious people are otherwise intelligent but all that means is that we need to explain how they can have such a large blind-spot.

Such explanations do not flatter the believer. One is that a kind of 'infantilism' 'lies behind the "need" for God'. In the preface of his book, Dawkins makes it clear that he chose the word 'delusion' knowing that it is used as a symptom of psychiatric disorder. Sam Harris writes, 'We have names for people who have many beliefs for which there is no rational justification. When their beliefs are extremely common, we call them "religious"; otherwise, they are likely to be called "mad", "psychotic" or "delusional". (Dawkins approvingly cites an almost identical quote from Robert Pirsig.)

Having discussed and debated religion with many intelligent people, I can't agree with this wilful equation of religious belief with insanity or stupidity. There is a sense in which all atheists do believe that religion is contrary to reason. But people do not generally believe that anyone who disagrees with them is simply irrational or stupid. We accept that reasonable people disagree about a wide range of matters and only throw around accusations of idiocy when the absence of rationality is egregious.

Nor is it the case that believers routinely ignore reason altogether, as suggested by Dawkins's remark that 'one of the truly bad effects of religion is that it teaches us that it is a virtue to be satisfied with not understanding'. I do think they are wrong, certainly, but they are not just being irrational in any uncontentious way. One common disagreement between believers and atheists is precisely about the proper limits of rationality and evidence in belief. The believer sees the atheist's refusal to believe in anything that is not established by the ordinary standards of argument and evidence as narrow-mindedness. Typically they will talk of the atheist needing to open up their hearts to God or being too confident that their standards of rationality are sufficient for understanding all the mysteries of existence. Their argument is that if religion seems irrational by your standards, that does not show that religion is irrational but that your conception of rationality is too narrow.

A good example of how competing conceptions of reason and its role clash can be seen in the so-called problem of evil. This is a simple but powerful argument against the existence of the traditional monotheistic God. God is supposed to be all-powerful, all-knowing, and all-loving. Yet there is avoidable suffering in the world. When we say 'avoidable' we do not just mean that it could be avoided if people acted differently. We also mean avoidable in the sense that a creator of the universe could have avoided such suffering ever coming to be. For example, there seems to be no reason why God could not have created a universe where extreme pain and particularly nasty diseases were not possible. He could also have made human minds more robust so that the lack of sympathy required to torture other people was not possible.

The existence of avoidable suffering in the world seems to be an undeniable fact. This must mean one of three things: God can't stop it, which means he is not all powerful; he doesn't want to stop it, so he isn't all-loving; or he doesn't know about it, which means he isn't all-knowing. Whichever option we take, the traditional Judaeo-Christian God can't exist.

Attempts to reconcile the existence of evil and God are known as theodicies. The most common is to argue that God can and wants to stop evil but doesn't because it is better for us in the long run that such suffering exists. Most of us find the explanations for this necessity wanting. How can it be necessary for anyone that thousands of people have been burned at the stake? But how much of a problem this is depends on how much you think it is reasonable to expect human beings to be able to understand the divine masterplan. It is entirely consistent for a believer to say, 'I can see that something like this must be true but I cannot imagine exactly how.'

For the atheist, the inability to provide a satisfactory answer to the problem of evil adds to the case against God's existence. For militant atheists, it is evidence that religious believers have effectively opted out of the usual standards of truth or falsity. Their refusal to be bothered by seeming contradictions shows that they are essentially irrational in their beliefs.

But if you think you have other good reasons to believe in God, not being able to account for everything does not necessarily make you irrational. For many believers, the existence of God is like the existence of time—they believe it exists even if its existence seems to generate logical paradoxes. For many centuries no one had a good answer to Zeno's arguments that it was logically impossible for an arrow in flight to ever actually be moving, or for Achilles, the fastest runner in Greece, to overtake a tortoise in a race. But rational people did not stop believing in time or space, or that arrows move and Achilles would overtake the tortoise. They simply accepted that they could not yet dissolve the contradictions.

So for many who believe in God, the problem of evil is a problem, not because it genuinely threatens to undermine their belief, but because it leaves them unable to explain what on the face of it looks inexplicable. But crucially, many religious believers would be prepared to live with the inexplicability of evil if they could not find a decent theodicy.

To say that reasonable people can disagree about the truth of religion is not to say that the arguments are finely balanced either way. There is a sense in which I do think that all rational people should be atheists. But since a good deal are not, it should be assumed that they are not simply being irrational and admit the possibility that there is something in what they believe that makes sense. It helps no one to simply stamp your foot and curse people's stupidity. Though, of course, I do that from time to time as well.

A general rule of intellectual debate is the principle of charity: try to put your opponent's arguments in the best possible light. Engage with the version of the argument that makes most rational sense, not the least. Similarly, assume your interlocutor has some intelligence unless proven otherwise. You should start with the assumption that there is no flagrant stupidity or disregard for rationality on either side and only give it up if you have to.

The principle of charity makes a natural bed-fellow for the principle of modesty: always be open to being wrong and never be overconfident about the power of your arguments no matter how strong they seem to you. Like children, ideas always seem better to those who have them.

When Dawkins says that the injunction of a theological college to 'think critically and biblically' is an oxymoron (GD 284) he is being too dismissive. A commitment to reason requires a proper modesty about the power of reason and our power to use it. We have to accept that there are no standards for judging what rationality demands which atheists and believers fully share.

Harmful religion

The second ground for being a more militant atheist is the claim that religion is harmful. The New Atheists make this claim very strongly. Although Dawkins says he never liked the title of his anti-religion television documentary *The Root of All Evil?*, his dislike wasn't strong enough to stop him going along with it. He certainly thinks it's the root of a lot of evil, saying that religion's 'wanton and carefully nurtured divisiveness . . . would be enough to make it a significant force for evil in the world'. (Given how divisive his approach is, this claim does seem a little ironic.) He also agrees with the Christian philosopher Blaise Pascal when he wrote, 'men never do evil so completely and cheerfully as when they do it from religious conviction'.

In what ways is religion supposed to be so uniquely pernicious? It cannot simply be that religion is wrong and belief in false things is inherently harmful. There is nothing harmful in itself in having what turns out to be a false scientific theory.

The claim that religions *always and necessarily* lead people to behave terribly doesn't stand up to scrutiny. If we were to tot up the atrocities committed by the faithful and the faithless, we could give pretty awful examples on both sides. Given that the world has been predominantly religious for millennia, more religious people would have done awful things simply because there have been more of them.

Religion has been accused of being damaging because it is life-denying rather than life-affirming, as Nietzsche argued. Religion encourages us to seek rewards in the illusory next world rather than in this one and therefore robs people of the motivation to make the most of the only life they have. But not all religious belief is life-denying. I'm reminded of the old slogan of the religious charity Christian Aid which proclaimed, 'We believe in life before death.' Certainly religions teach a certain amount of restraint, but so do all ethical systems. And it certainly seems that many religious believers do lead full and happy lives.

Another objection to religion popular among the New Atheists is that most extremism is motivated by religious faith, such as the contemporary terrorism conducted in the name of Islam and the historical Christian inquisitions and crusades. Although not all religion is this extreme, they argue that you cannot separate out religion's harmful effects from its more benign ones. Certainly if you turn up at a typical Church of England Sunday morning service you won't find anything too objectionable. But moderate religious belief is part of a network of belief that includes more harmful fundamentalism. 'Even mild and moderate religion helps to provide the climate of faith in which extremism naturally flourishes,' argues Dawkins. 'The teachings of "moderate" religion, though not extremist in themselves, are an open invitation to extremism.' It is just an illusion to think that moderate religious belief can exist without its extremist wings. Even if it could, fundamentalism needs moderate religion because it provides the soil of acceptability in which the otherwise unacceptable can grow.

I think there is something to this, but I am concerned that the same argument could apply to any belief which comes in moderate and extreme forms. For instance, there are huge differences between democratic socialism and state communism, or peacefully being against abortion and murdering doctors who carry out abortion. Reasonable beliefs should not be made guilty by mere association with mindless prejudices or extremism.

The case that religion is essentially and especially harmful is weak and therefore so is the belief that the falsity of religion is enough to justify militant opposition to it. At root, though, opposition to militant atheism can be based on a commitment to the very values that most atheists say inspire them: an open-minded commitment to rational enquiry and truth. These are rightly called values because they express claims not only about what is true but about what we feel to be most important. Hostile opposition to the beliefs of others combined with a dogged conviction of the certainty of one's own beliefs is antithetical to such values. Reason and argument are not just tools to be used to win over converts. They are processes that need to be engaged with and to engage in them with other people one needs to be open to their alternative viewpoints. They cannot be engaged with properly if they are seen as battering rams to destroy the edifice of religious belief.

Missing the point

Atheist critiques of religion are often accused of missing the point. As the cultural theorist Terry Eagleton put it, listening to an atheist talk theology is sometimes comparable to 'someone holding forth on biology whose only knowledge of the subject is the Book of British Birds'.

Richard Dawkins challenged this by dismissing the idea that there was any legitimate expertise in religion that a person could lack. He argued that you need no more be a theologian to know that religion is nonsense than you need to be a 'fairyologist' to know fairies don't exist. Whether this refutes or proves Eagleton's point is a matter of debate. It hasn't stopped versions of this argument against the New Atheism becoming extremely popular. The general point is that the New Atheists attack only the crudest, most simplistic and literal forms of religious belief. Having destroyed their straw men they fail to notice that more serious religion has been unscathed by their withering attacks.

One such line of argument has been popularized by Karen Armstrong. She argues that there is a distinction between *logos*, the kind of literal truth pursued by scientists and historians, and *mythos*, the non-literal truth of literature, poetry, and religion. The New Atheists' mistake is to attack religion as though it were concerned with *logos*. As Dawkins says, '"the God Hypothesis" is a scientific hypothesis about the universe, which should be analysed as sceptically as any other'.

A similar separation of science and religion is made by the biologist Stephen Jay Gould who argued that each has its own magisterium, a domain over which it has authority. The magisterium of science 'covers the empirical realm: what the Universe is made of (fact) and why does it work in this way (theory). The magisterium of religion extends over questions of ultimate meaning and moral value. These two magisteria do not overlap, nor do they encompass all inquiry.' Gould refers to his theory of 'non-overlapping magisteria' by the acronym NOMA.

Clearly there are many religious people who do not see God as a literal entity or sacred texts as historical documents. One such person is the non-realist theologian Don Cupitt. For Cupitt, religion provides a unique and invaluable way of orientating oneself to life and its mysteries. It employs concepts like 'god' and 'divine', but in the modern world we don't have to believe they refer to anything objectively real. Religion is a 'form of life', to use Wittgenstein's terminology. Or, as sociologists say, it is an 'imaginary', meaning the symbolic system through which we create our ways of representing our collective life and values.

However, it is questionable to put it mildly whether this is indeed how religious believers usually understand their faith, even if you believe it is how religion ought properly to be understood. The stripping away of any claims religion makes about the nature of reality seems to be confined to the margins of most faiths. A recent authoritative Gallup survey suggests 24 per cent of all Americans, not just Christians, believe that the Bible is 'the actual word of God, and is to be taken literally, word for word', while 26 per cent view it as 'a book of fables, legends, history and moral precepts recorded by man'. In Britain, 31 per cent of all Christians believe the Bible version of Christ's resurrection word for word, rising to 57 per cent of those who go to a religious service at least once a month. The likes of Cupitt exist, but they are on the margins of mainstream religion, under fire from both Christians and atheists.

So while it is true that the form of religion most attacked by the New Atheists is literal and simplistic, it is wishful thinking by the more theologically sophisticated to believe that this is not as a matter of fact just the kind of religion that is most widely professed.

Some New Atheists also question how rigorously apparently sophisticated believers maintain their distinctions between scientific and religious truth. In my experience, almost every time I press an apparently liberal Christian on whether they think Jesus died on the cross and that was that, they acknowledge that they not only believe something truly exceptional did happen afterwards, but that if it didn't, their faith would lie in tatters.

Dawkins also accuses advocates of NOMA of having double standards. He asks us to 'imagine, by some remarkable set of circumstances, that forensic archaeologists unearthed DNA evidence to show that Jesus really did lack a biological father. Can you imagine religious apologists shrugging their shoulders and saying . . . "Who cares? Scientific evidence is completely irrelevant to theological questions."'

Dawkins's complaint reflects a wider feature of the somewhat tired science versus religion debate. It should now be obvious that religion and science are perfectly compatible, just as long as your version of religion does not rely on any unscientific claims, such as the denial of evolution or belief in immaterial souls. Fidelity to something like NOMA is required. But too often the religious can't resist treading on science's toes, arguing that in some way science points to the truth of their faith. This usually involves the more mysterious corners of physics, such as dark matter or quantum indeterminacy. Such arguments are generally sophisticated dressing-ups of the claim that since there are mysteries in science, the existence of a mysterious God is at worst perfectly possible and at best made more probable.

The New Atheists are not guilty of erecting a straw man when they attack the quasi-scientific claims of many religious believers. However, if you demolish the literal beliefs of the major monotheistic religions, that is not necessarily the end of them. Religion may *usually* involve wrong beliefs, but it is not just about belief. It is also about practice, ritual, community, ways of orientating ourselves to the mysteries of the universe. These are debates New Atheism has not even engaged in, dismissing them as irrelevant side-shows.

Atheism has always been more heterogeneous than the New Atheism would suggest. Today, alongside the moderate–militant spectrum is a continuum running from those who think religion should be consigned to history and those who think that there is still a lot to gain by engaging with less literalist forms of religion. There could even be a lot of common ground in a shared respect for taking life seriously, seeking meaning and purpose, living with mystery, humility, and gratitude. Alain de Botton's *Religion for Atheists* (2012) is an example of this. Even the New Atheist Sam Harris has written about the truths to be found in certain spiritual traditions, notably Buddhism, in his *Waking Up: Searching for*

Spirituality Without Religion (2015). The overwhelmingly pugilistic tone introduced by the New Atheism has receded somewhat, making space for atheists more sympathetic to religion to reclaim their central place in the atheist family.

Downhill from now on?

Various people have claimed for different reasons that the relative flourishing of atheism in the West over recent centuries is a temporary aberration and that the future belongs to the faithful.

There are two broad families of arguments for this. One makes no value judgements and is based on pure demography. In *Shall the Religious Inherit the Earth?* (2010), Eric Kaufmann answers his titular question in the affirmative. The basic argument is simple. The more societies become secularized, the fewer children people have. In many countries today, reproduction rates are below replacement levels, meaning that without immigration populations will decline. In religious societies and communities, however, the fertility rates are much higher. Evangelical Christians and Orthodox Jews have on average more children than others in the nations in which they live, while birth rates in majority Muslim countries are higher than in secular ones. To put it crudely, the religious will outbreed the non-religious.

Many assumptions need to be made to turn observed demographic data of recent years into future projections. Most obviously, it is assumed that children will have the same beliefs as their parents. If that were a general truth, we wouldn't have seen the growth of atheism in the first place. Still, the demographic argument points to how atheism has no future unless it can persuade people that it offers a positive, better alternative to religion.

The second family of arguments for the decline of atheism claims it is incapable of providing such an alternative. For example, Alister McGrath argues that atheism's 'golden age'—from the fall of the Bastille in 1789 to the fall of the Berlin wall 200 years later—is over. Human beings have spiritual needs that we are discovering atheism cannot serve. Atheist societies rely on a morality that, as Nietzsche argued, has no basis without Christianity. And so on. McGrath's argument that atheism is going to wane is in essence an argument that it is intellectually and morally bankrupt. On this, of course, there is much disagreement and this book has offered several rejoinders to the charge.

The evidence of atheism's actual decline, however, is weak. For a start, there is no high peak for it to decline from. Throughout the so-called golden age atheists have been a small minority. This has been a period of secularism, of state neutrality in religion, but not of widespread disbelief. The narrative of decline is therefore premised on a fictional prior incline. What's more, since McGrath wrote his book atheism has continued to grow in the most religious developed Western society, the United States.

Only time will tell if atheism is on an upward or downward trajectory. But it is not our main task to predict which path it will follow. We should be deciding whether it is both true and practical. If it is neither or both then we would have good reasons to resist it. Otherwise, we would have every reason to desire a more atheist future, whether or not it comes about.

I hope this book helps you to make your own, informed decision.

Further reading

Chapter 1: What is atheism?

Robin Gordon Brown and James Ladyman, *Materialism: A Historical and Philosophical Inquiry* (Routledge, 2019)

Tim Crane, *The Meaning of Belief: Religion from an Atheist's Point of View* (Harvard University Press, 2017)

Alex Rosenberg, *The Atheist's Guide to Reality* (W. W. Norton & Co., 2012)

Gilbert Ryle, *The Concept of Mind* (Hutchinson, 1949)

Chapter 2: The case for atheism

O. Blanke and S. Arzy, 'The Out-of-Body Experience: Disturbed Self-Processing at the Temporo-Parietal Junction'. *The Neuroscientist*, 11 (1) (2005), 16–24

Richard Dawkins, *The Blind Watchmaker* (W. W. Norton, 1986)

David Hume, *An Enquiry Concerning Human Understanding* (1748)

David Hume, *Dialogues Concerning Natural Religion* (1779)

Søren Kierkegaard, *Fear and Trembling* (1843)

Stephen Law, *Humanism: A Very Short Introduction* (Oxford University Press, 2011)

Michael P. Lynch, *In Praise of Reason* (MIT Press, 2012)

Blaise Pascal, *Pensées* (1660)

Robin le Poidevin, *Arguing for Atheism* (Routledge, 1996)

Bertrand Russell, *Why I am Not a Christian* (George Allen and Unwin, 1957)

Chapter 3: Atheist ethics

Aristotle, *Nicomachean Ethics* (*c.*340 BCE)
Patricia Churchland, *Conscience: The Origins of Moral Intuition* (W. W. Norton, 2019)
Confucius, *The Analects* (*c.*479–221 BCE)
Carol Gilligan, *In a Different Voice: Psychological Theory and Women's Development* (Harvard University Press, 1982)
David Hume, *An Enquiry Concerning the Principles of Morals* (1751)
Immanuel Kant, *Groundwork of the Metaphysics of Morals* (1785)
John Stuart Mill, *Utilitarianism* (1861)
Plato, *Euthyphro* (*c.*399–390 BCE)
Jean-Paul Sartre, *Existentialism and Humanism* (Methuen, 1948)
Peter Singer (ed.), *A Companion to Ethics* (Blackwell, 1991)
Adam Smith, *The Theory of Moral Sentiments* (1759)
Nick Spencer, *The Evolution of the West: How Christianity Has Shaped our Values* (SPCK, 2016)

Chapter 4: Meaning and purpose

Ray Bradbury, *The Martian Chronicles* (Rupert Hart-Davis, 1951)
Albert Camus, *The Myth of Sisyphus* (Hamish Hamilton, 1955)
Richard Dawkins, *The Selfish Gene*, 2nd edition (Oxford University Press, 1989)
Viktor Frankl, *Man's Search for Meaning* (Beacon Press, 1959)
Todd May, *A Fragile Life* (Chicago University Press, 2017)
Thomas Nagel, *Mortal Questions* (Cambridge University Press, 1979)
Friedrich Nietzsche, *On The Genealogy of Morals* (1887)

Chapter 5: Atheism in history

David Berman, *A History of Atheism in Britain* (Routledge, 1988)
Philipp Blom, *A Wicked Company: The Forgotten Radicalism of the European Enlightenment* (Basic Books, 2012)
Andrew Copson, *Secularism: A Very Short Introduction* (Oxford University Press, 2019)
Philip J. Ivanhoe and Bryan W. Van Norden (eds), *Readings in Classical Chinese Philosophy*, 2nd edition (Hackett, 2005)
James Thrower, *Western Atheism: A Short History* (Prometheus Books, 2000)
Tim Whitmarsh, *Battling the Gods* (Faber & Faber, 2016)

Bernard Williams, *Truth and Truthfulness* (Princeton University Press, 2002)

Robert Wuthnow (ed.), *The Encyclopedia of Politics and Religion* (Routledge, 1998). See especially the entries on 'Atheism' by Paul G. Crowley (pp. 48–54), 'Fascism' by Roger Griffin (pp. 257–64), 'Germany' by Uwe Berndt (pp. 299–302), 'Holocaust' by Kristen Renwick Monroe (pp. 334–42), 'Italy' by Alberto Melloni (pp. 399–404), 'Papacy' by R. Scott Appelby (pp. 590–5), 'Russia' by Michael Bordeaux (pp. 655–8), 'Spain' by William Callahan (pp. 711–14)

Chapter 6: Atheism in the 21st century

Scott F. Aikin and Robert B. Talisse, *Reasonable Atheism: A Moral Case for Reasonable Disbelief* (Prometheus Books, 2011)

Karen Armstrong, *The Case for God: What Religion Really Means* (Bodley Head, 2009)

Don Cupitt, *The Sea of Faith*, 2nd edition (SCM Press, 1994)

Richard Dawkins, *The God Delusion* (Bantam, 2006)

Daniel C. Dennett, *Darwin's Dangerous Idea* (Simon & Schuster, 1995)

Daniel C. Dennett, *Breaking the Spell: Religion as a Natural Phenomenon* (Viking, 2006)

John Gray, *Seven Types of Atheism* (Allen Lane, 2018)

Sam Harris, *The End of Faith* (W. W. Norton, 2004)

Christopher Hitchens, *God Is Not Great* (Hachette, 2007)

Stephen Jay Gould, *Rock of Ages* (Random House, 1999)

Eric Kaufmann, *Shall the Religious Inherit the Earth?* (Profile, 2010)

Alister McGrath, *The Twilight of Atheism* (Doubleday, 2004)

Michel Onfray, *In Defence of Atheism Manifesto: The Case Against Christianity, Judaism, and Islam* (Serpent's Tail, 2005)

Alvin Plantinga, *Where the Conflict Really Lies: Science, Religion, and Naturalism* (Oxford University Press, 2012)

Index

For the benefit of digital users, indexed terms that span two pages (e.g., 52–53) may, on occasion, appear on only one of those pages.

AGNOSTICISM
A Very Short Introduction
Robin Le Poidevin

What is agnosticism? Is it just the 'don't know' position on God, or is there more to it than this? Is it a belief, or merely the absence of belief? Who were the first to call themselves 'agnostics'? These are just some of the questions that Robin Le Poidevin considers in this *Very Short Introduction*. He sets the philosophical case for agnosticism and explores it as a historical and cultural phenomenon. What emerges is a much more sophisticated, and much more interesting, attitude than a simple failure to either commit to, or reject, religious belief. Le Poidevin challenges some preconceptions and assumptions among both believers and non-atheists, and invites the reader to rethink their own position on the issues.

www.oup.com/vsi

Humanism
A Very Short Introduction
Stephen Law

Religion is currently gaining a much higher profile. The number of faith schools is increasingly, and religious points of view are being aired more frequently in the media. As religion's profile rises, those who reject religion, including humanists, often find themselves misunderstood, and occasionally misrepresented. Stephen Law explores how humanism uses science and reason to make sense of the world, looking at how it encourages individual moral responsibility and shows that life can have meaning without religion. Challenging some of the common misconceptions, he seeks to dispute the claims that atheism and humanism are 'faith positions' and that without God there can be no morality and our lives are left without purpose.

www.oup.com/vsi

ISLAMIC HISTORY
A Very Short Introduction
Adam J. Silverstein

Does history matter? This book argues not that history matters, but that Islamic history does. This *Very Short Introduction* introduces the story of Islamic history; the controversies surrounding its study; and the significance that it holds - for Muslims and for non-Muslims alike. Opening with a lucid overview of the rise and spread of Islam, from the seventh to twenty first century, the book charts the evolution of what was originally a small, localised community of believers into an international religion with over a billion adherents. Chapters are also dedicated to the peoples - Arabs, Persians, and Turks - who shaped Islamic history, and to three representative institutions - the mosque, jihad, and the caliphate - that highlight Islam's diversity over time.

'The book is extremely lucid, readable, sensibly organised, and wears its considerable learning, as they say, 'lightly'.'

BBC History Magazine

www.oup.com/vsi

PAGANISM
A Very Short Introduction
Owen Davies

This *Very Short Introduction* explores the meaning of paganism - through a chronological overview of the attitudes towards its practices and beliefs - from the ancient world through to the present day. Owen Davies largely looks at paganism through the eyes of the Christian world, and how, over the centuries, notions and representations of its nature were shaped by religious conflict, power struggles, colonialism, and scholarship. Despite the expansion of Christianity and Islam, Pagan cultures continue to exist around the world, whilst in the West new formations of paganism constitute one of the fastest-growing religions.

www.oup.com/vsi

RELIGION IN AMERICA
A Very Short Introduction
Timothy Beal

Timothy Beal describes many aspects of religion in contemporary America that are typically ignored in other books on the subject, including religion in popular culture and counter-cultural groups; the growing phenomenon of "hybrid" religious identities, both individual and collective; the expanding numbers of new religious movements, or NRMs, in America; and interesting examples of "outsider religion." He also offers an engaging overview of the history of religion in America, from Native American traditions to the present day. Finally, Beal highlights the three major forces shaping the present and future of religion in America.

www.oup.com/vsi

SCIENCE AND RELIGION
A Very Short Introduction
Thomas Dixon

The debate between science and religion is never out of the news: emotions run high, fuelled by polemical bestsellers and, at the other end of the spectrum, high-profile campaigns to teach 'Intelligent Design' in schools. Yet there is much more to the debate than the clash of these extremes. As Thomas Dixon shows in this balanced and thought-provoking introduction, many have seen harmony rather than conflict between faith and science. He explores not only the key philosophical questions that underlie the debate, but also the social, political, and ethical contexts that have made 'science and religion' such a fraught and interesting topic in the modern world, offering perspectives from non-Christian religions and examples from across the physical, biological, and social sciences.

'A rich introductory text . . . on the study of relations of science and religion.'

R. P. Whaite, Metascience